C000196199

Liverpool Everyman & Playhouse present the world première of

THE STAR
The Big Brilliant Musical Hall Show
An Entertainment by Michael Wynne

First performed at the Liverpool Playhouse on 9 Dec 2016

LIVERPOOL EVERYMAN & PLAYHOUSE

Two Great Theatres.
One Creative Heart.

**We are two distinct theatres, almost a mile apart,
which together make up a single artistic force.**

For over 10 years we have been driven by our passion for our art-form, our love of our city and our unswerving belief that theatre at its best can enhance lives. While our two performance bases could hardly be more different, they are united by our commitment to brilliant, humane, forward-thinking theatre that responds to its time and place.

Our mission is to reflect the aspirations and concerns of our audiences, to dazzle and inspire them, welcome and connect with them, nurture the artists within them and fuel their civic pride. Wherever these connections happen – whether in our theatres, in the community, in schools, or outside Liverpool – we hope to ignite the imagination, explore what it is to be human and always to exceed expectation.

From 2017 a resident acting company returns to the Everyman. The Company will comprise of 14 actors, a team of three designers and in-house directors Gemma Bodinetz, Nick Bagnall and Matt Rutter. The theatre will become a place of change and diversity that welcomes people from all backgrounds to enhance and develop their skills. From February to July they will perform *Fiddler on the Roof, The Conquest of the South Pole, The Story Giant, The Sum* and *Romeo and Juliet.*

To find out more about the Liverpool Everyman & Playhouse work, both on and off stage, call **0151 709 4776** visit **www.everymanplayhouse.com**
or follow **@LivEveryPlay** on Twitter

Liverpool Everyman & Playhouse are a registered charity (1081229) and gratefully acknowledge the support of our funders, donors and audiences.

For their ongoing financial support, we would like to thank:

Andrew Lloyd Webber Foundation, Esmée Fairbairn Foundation, Foyle Foundation, Garfield Weston Foundation, Gilbert-Ash, JP Getty Jnr Charitable Trust, John Ellerman Foundation, The Monument Trust, The Oglesby Charitable Trust, Paul Hamlyn Foundation

Our Principal Partner:

Liverpool John Moores University

Our Business Members and Sponsors:

Benson Signs, Bolland & Lowe, Bruntwood, Duncan Sheard Glass, EEF, Exterion Media, Hope Street Hotel, Knowsley Chamber of Commerce, LA Productions, Liverpool City Region LEP, Liverpool and Sefton Chamber of Commerce, Morecrofts Solicitors, NW Systems Group, Professional Liverpool, Rathbone Investment Management, Synergy, Wrightsure Insurance Group

Our Patrons:
Hilary Banner, Robin Bloxsidge, Hilary Fass, Penny and Charles Feeny, Sean Harrington, Brian Higgins, Michael Moore, Wendy Owen, Max Stone, Paul Vaight

Those who have left us a legacy:
Dorothy Smellie
Anni Parker & Brian Barry, lovers and supporters of theatre
Malcolm and Roger Frood in memory of Graham and Joan Frood

And all the individual donors listed on our website at
www.everymanplayhouse.com

Credits

Cast (in alphabetical order)

Eithne Browne	Ellen
Michelle Butterly	Ida
Helen Carter	Dora
Kevin Harvey	Mr Charles
Danny O'Brien	Arthur Crown
Jack Rigby	Jack
Michael Starke	The Chairman

Other parts played by members of the company

James Breckon	Musician
Elliot Chapman	Musician
Danny Miller	Musician

Company

Writer	**Michael Wynne**
Director	**Philip Wilson**
Designer	**Matthew Wright**
Arranger & Musical Director	**Alex Smith**
Lighting Designer	**Johanna Town**
Sound Designer	**John Leonard**
Choreographer	**Cressida Carré**
Magic Consultant	**John Bulleid**
Assistant Director	**Jack Cooper**
Casting Consultant	**Kay Magson CDG**
Costume Supervisor	**Fi Carrington & Jacquie Davies**
Wardrobe Deputy	**Laura Hollowell**
Production Manager	**Ali Fowler**
Company Managers	**Sarah Lewis & Gemma Dunne**
Stage Manager	**Katie Bosomworth**
Deputy Stage Manager	**Steph Carter**
Assistant Stage Manager	**Jacob Amos**
Lighting Programmer	**Gareth Hughes**
Lighting Operator	**Lorraine Marshall**
Stage Technicians	**Mike Gray & Howard Macaulay**
Sound Engineer	**Xenia Bayer**
Sound No.2	**Phil Ronayne**
Followspot Operators	**Dominic Phillips & Vaughan Taylor**
Dresser	**Anna Souter**
Scenic Construction	**Splinter**
Scenic Artists	**Dartura Art & Design**

Michael Wynne would like to thank Alan Stocks, Mark Arends, Pauline Daniels, Greg Last, Lindsay Rodden, Hayley Greggs, Moira Callaghan and Ken Dodd.

The production would like to thank Prompt Side Ltd.

EITHNE BROWNE
Ellen

Eithne is so happy to be back on stage at the Playhouse as this is the place her career started in Willy Russell's *Blood Brothers*. From chorus girl to leading lady a varied career has followed and listed below are a few highlights...

Theatre credits include: *Tartuffe, Awfully Big Adventure, The Odd Couple, Blood Brothers* (Liverpool Playhouse); *I am Janet* (Theatre Gap); *Mam! I'm 'Ere!, Night Collar, Special Measures, Ladies Day, A Fistful of Collars, Funny Money, Merry Ding Dong, Dirty Dusting, Lost Soul, Eight Miles High, Cinderella, Two, Brick up the Mersey Tunnel* (Royal Court); *Boeing Boeing, Intent to Murder, Say Who You Are* (Vienna's English Theatre); *Home Fires* (Dukes, Lancaster); *Talking Heads* (CTTC Productions); *Eight Miles High, Pocket Dream, Alfie* (Bolton Octagon); *To Kill a Mocking Bird* (New Vic, Stoke); *The Full Monty* (Drop Nothing Ltd); *The Secret Garden* (The Byre, St Andrews); *Cinderella* (Floral Pavilion, New Brighton); *Limestone Cowboy* (Coventry Belgrade); *Wuthering Heights, Educating Rita, Abigail's Party* (National Tour); *Month in the Country, Billy Liar* (Salisbury Playhouse); *Shirley Valentine* (Northcott, Exeter); *Breezeblock Park* (Queens, Hornchurch) and *Stags and Hens* (Young Vic).

Television and film credits include: *The Johnny and Inel Show* (CBBC); *Hollyoaks* (Lime Pictures); *Coup* (Company Pictures); *Room at the Top* (Great Meadows Productions); *Warriors, The Marksman* (BBC); *Mobile* (ITV); *The Royal IV, Emmerdale* (YTV); *Having it Off, Clocking Off* (Red Productions); *Cold Feet, Brookside* (Mersey Television); *and Business as Usual* (Cannon Films).

Radio credits include: *The Immaculate Conception, In Loving Memory* (BBC) and *Secrets in Sepia* (Watershed Partnership).

These performances are dedicated to Kitty Grant. Thanks to Roger Appleton for support in research and development. And now, sit, sing, enjoy!

MICHELLE BUTTERLY
Ida

Michelle trained at Central School of Speech and Drama.

Theatre credits include: *Hope Place, Dead Heavy Fantastic* (Everyman, Liverpool); *A Streetcar Named Desire, Hamlet* (Royal Exchange, Manchester); *Everyman* (National Theatre); *Noughts and Crosses, Speaking Like Magpies, A New Way to Please You, Believe What You Will, Thomas More* (Royal Shakespeare Company); *A Servant to Two Masters* (Royal Shakespeare Company/Young Vic/West End); *Blair's Children* (Cockpit); *Queen of the Nile* (Hull Truck); *One for the Road* (Royal Theatre Northampton); *Ma Via En Rose* (Young Vic); *I Like Mine With a Kiss* (Bush); *Gone to Earth* (Shared Experience); *The People Are Friendly* (Royal Court); *Road, Shakers* (Wolsey Ipswich); *Peggy Buck, Lent* (Belgrade Coventry); *End of the Food Chain* (Stephen Joseph); *Laundry Room at the Hotel Madrid* (Gate) and *Gaslight* (Theatr Clwyd).

Television credits include: *Little Boy Blue, Doctors, Benidorm* (Series regular), *Beautiful People, Midsomer Murders, Minder, No Angels, Eyes Down, Dangerfield, Pie in the Sky, Hetty Wainthropp Investigates, Soldier Soldier* (Series regular), *St Clare, The Echo, Heartbeat and Casualty* (Series regular).

Film credits include: *Hamlet and Chromophobia.*

Radio credits include: *What Does the K Stand for?* and *Death of a Pirate.*

HELEN CARTER
Dora

Helen trained at LAMDA.

Theatre credits include: *Dead Heavy Fantastic* (Everyman, Liverpool); *No Wise Men, Once Upon a Time at the Adelphi, The Flint Street Nativity* (Liverpool Playhouse); *Father O'Flaherty Saves Our Souls, Mam! I'm 'Ere!, Scouse of the Antarctic, Slappers and Slapheads,* (Royal Court, Liverpool); *The Sunshine Boys, The Last 5 Years* (Life in Theatre); *Word:play* (Box of Tricks); *The Gatekeeper* (Royal Exchange Manchester); *Top Girls* (Royal Court, London); *No Wise Men, Dad's Army Marches On* (Tour) and *The Honest Whore* (Globe Theatre).

Television credits include: *Wallander* (Left Bank Pictures); *Doctors, Judge John Deed* (BBC); *Beaten* (Coastal Productions) and *A470* (S4C).

Film credits include: *96 Ways to Say I Love You* (Daisy Aitkens and Georgia Tennant).

KEVIN HARVEY
Mr Charles

Theatre credits include: *The Alchemist* (Liverpool Playhouse); *Tis Pity She's a Whore* (Everyman, Liverpool) *Tartuffe* (Everyman, Liverpool & Rose Kingston); *Yellowman* (Everyman, Liverpool & Hampstead Theatre);*The Bakkhai, Game* (Almeida Theatre); *The Book of Mormon* (Sonia Friedman Prods); *Titus Andronicus, Candide, Speaking Like Magpies, Sejanus: His Fall, Believe What You Will, Thomas Moore* (RSC); *Decade* (Headlong); *Tiny Volcanoes* (Paines Plough); *Salt* (Royal Exchange Manchester); *Wig Out* (Royal Court Theatre); *Stags & Hens* (Royal Court, Liverpool); *Chapter 21* (Breaking Cycles/National Theatre); *Dr. Faustus* (Bristol Old Vic); *Macbeth* (Out of Joint); *The Key Game* (Talawa) and *Ragamuffin* (UKArts).

Television and film credits include: *The Jury* (Dragonfly Films); *Safe House 2* (11th Hour/ITV); *Prey Series 2* (Red Productions); *Good Cop, Paradox, Spooks: Code 9, The Adam & Shelley Show, The Ruby in the Smoke* (BBC); *Ding Dong* (Sky); *A Boy Called Dad* (Wonderboy Ltd); *Salvage* (Digital Departures); *Til Death* (Signature Pictures) and *Everybody Loves Sunshine* (Channel 4 Films).

Radio credits include: *Stone: Sexting, Threepenny Opera, Words and Music, Cavalry, Brief Lives, Fused Ricebowl, The Book of Love, The Morning After, Why Don't You Stop Talking* (BBC) and *Just a Girl* (Naked Productions).

DANNY O'BRIEN
Arthur Crown

This is Danny's first time at the Playhouse, he has been working around the North West and Europe for the last few years.

Theatre credits include: *Lost Soul, Stags and Hens, The Rainbow Connection, The Salon, One Night in Istanbul* (European tour), *Noises Off, Rita Sue and Bob too, The King of Edge Hill, Bouncers* and *Pharaoh Cross the Mersey* (Royal Court, Liverpool).

Television and film credits include: *Good Cop* and *Scrims*.

Daniel would like to dedicate his performance to his two daughters Pearl and Edie.

JACK RIGBY
Jack

Jack made his stage debut at the age of 11 years performing in an amateur production of *Our Day Out* at the Neptune Theatre, Liverpool. Some years later he was cast in the newly revamped musical version directed by Willy Russell at the Royal Court, Liverpool. Jack trained and graduated from LIPA, gaining a BA (Hons) Degree in Acting (2012).

Television and film credits include: *Mobile* (ITV); *Waterloo Road* (BBC); *Don't Worry About Me; Small Creatures; The Be All and End All; Pleasure Island* (2015); *Arthur and Merlin* (2015).

Theatre credits include: *Macbeth, A Midsummer Night's Dream, Our Day Out, Hitchhiker's guide to Fazakerley* (Royal Court, Liverpool) and *Cinderella* (St Helen's Theatre Royal).

MICHAEL STARKE
The Chairman

Michael began his professional career on stage at Liverpool Playhouse in the 1984 production of *Cavern of Dreams*, by Carol Ann Duffy. Michael is probably best known to TV viewers as Sinbad, a role he played for fifteen years in Channel 4's *Brookside*. He was in six series of Yorkshire TV's *The Royal* playing Ken Hopkirk, and played Jerry Morton in *Coronation Street*, as well as episodes of *Doctors* and *Holby* (BBC).

Theatre credits include: *The Resistible Rise of Arturo Ui, Hamlet, The Winter's Tale, The Taming of the Shew, She Stoops to Conquer, Three Sisters, No Holds Bard* (Everyman, Liverpool); *Be Bop A Lula, Blood Brothers* (Leicester Haymarket); *Anything Goes, Sister Act, Hairspray* (National Tour); *The Rocky Horror Picture Show* (Liverpool Empire); *The Play What I Wrote* (Kenneth Branagh); *Sons of the Desert, Shed, Bouncers, Lucky Numbers, Our Day Out, Nightmare on Lime Street, Hitchikers Guide to Fazakerley, Scouse of the Antarctic* and *Pharaoh Cross the Mersey* (Royal Court, Liverpool).

Television and film credits include: *Shadow Recruit* (Jack Ryan); *No Surrender* (Alan Bleasdale); *Distant Voices* (Terence Davies) and *The 51st State* (Ronny Yu).

Michael would like to dedicate his performance to the memories of David Graham, Mickey Finn, Chris Finley and Herbert Howe. All 'Stars' that shared this stage.

JAMES BRECKON
Musician

James is a 21 year old professional keyboard player, recently graduated from The Liverpool Institute for Performing Arts. He sessions for pop bands (including tours throughout UK, US, Canada, Spain and Japan with 80's sensations China Crisis, Natalie McCool and Spanish artist Julian Maeso), as well as regularly playing functions, weddings, musical theatre (with the last show playing to an audience of over 14,000 people), holds cocktail piano residencies and composes, which has taken him around the country and onto national television.

James is currently working as a cocktail pianist at the Richmond Hotel in Liverpool and is Musical Director for Polka Dot Pantomimes. He is a freelance audition pianist, for such companies as Norwegian Cruise Line and Pearson Castings. His composition works have been featured in The Liverpool Echo, commissions for Rambert School of Dance and James is currently working on his first Television composition credit.

ELLIOT CHAPMAN
Musician

Elliot is originally from Lancashire and trained at The Liverpool Institute for Performing Arts where he graduated with BA (Hons) in Music specialising in Session Musicianship. Alongside the musical theatre work he teaches in schools in the North West, he is currently working with a diverse range of Professional bands around the North of England. He has performed in many different venues across the North West such as Bridgewater Hall Manchester, King Georges Hall Blackburn, Epstein Theatre Liverpool, Burnley Mechanics Theatre, Preston Guildhall and The Grand theatre Clitheroe.

Theatre credits include: *Shout! The Mod Musical* (Royal Court, Liverpool); *Tick, Tick, Boom!, Little Shop of Horros, Bugsy Malone, Annie* and *We Will Rock You* (Edinburgh Fringe Festival August 2015).

DANNY MILLER
Musician

Originally from the North East, Danny took up the trumpet at an early age, later learning the bass guitar. Danny graduated from The Liverpool Institute for Performing Arts with a 1st in the summer of 2016. He is currently musical director of 9 piece New Orleans style band Hardcore Hornography, 3 piece brass section, The Horn Supremacy and the 19 piece Close Enough For Jazz Big Band.

MICHAEL WYNNE
Writer

Michael Wynne is an Olivier Award winning playwright. His first play, *The Knocky*, was performed at the Royal Court Theatre and the Everyman, Liverpool - and was awarded the Meyer Whitworth Award for Best New Play and Liverpool Echo Arts Award for Best New Talent.

Theatre credits include: *Hope Place* and *The Knocky* (Everyman, Liverpool); *Who Cares, The Priory* (Olivier Award, Best New Comedy), *The People are Friendly, The Red Flag, Friday Night Sex* (Royal Court, London); *Sell Out, Dirty Wonderland* (Frantic Assembly); *The Boy Who Left Home* (Actor Touring Company); *Tits/Teeth* (Soho Theatre/NYT) and *Canvas* (Chichester).

Television credits include: *Being Eileen, Lapland, Substance, Eyes Down, UGetMe, Mayo* (BBC); *Little Crackers/Sheridan Smith/ The Daltons* (Sky1); *Grafters, Where The Heart Is, Don't Eat the Neighbours* (ITV), *As If* and *Sugar Rush* (Channel 4).

Film credits include: *My Summer of Love* - BAFTA for Best British Film, Evening Standard Film Award for Best Screenplay, The Michael Powell Award for Best British Film at the Edinburgh Film Festival.

PHILIP WILSON
Director

Philip is the former Artistic Director of Salisbury Playhouse (2007-11).

Theatre credits include: *The Norman Conquests*; *Noises Off*; *Dr Faustus* and *The Astonished Heart/Still Life* (Liverpool Playhouse); *The Game of Love and Chance, The Constant Wife, The Picture, Private Lives, Arsenic and Old Lace, The Winslow Boy,* his own adaptation of JL Carr's *A Month in the Country, What the Butler Saw, People at Sea, Alphabetical Order, Corpse!, Blackbird, Faith Healer, Toro! Toro!* (Salisbury Playhouse); *As You Like It* (Storyhouse, Chester); *Beacons* (Park Theatre, London); his own adaptations of Philip Pullman's *Grimm Tales* (Oxo Tower Bargehouse & Shoreditch Town Hall, London); *The Three Lions* (St. James Theatre, Edinburgh & UK Tour); *How Many Miles to Babylon?* (Lyric Belfast); *Toro! Toro!* (National tour); *Twist of Gold* (Polka, London); the books of Ruth and 2 Samuel in *Sixty-Six Books* (Bush Theatre, London & Westminster Abbey); *The Importance of Being Earnest/Travesties* (Birmingham Rep); *If Love Were All* and *In Praise Of Love* (Minerva, Chichester); *The Found Man* (Traverse, Edinburgh); *Un Uomo Trovato* (Teatro della Limonaia, Florence); *Ain't Misbehavin'* (Sheffield Crucible) and *Breaking The Code* (Theatre Royal, Northampton).

Philip spent two years as a producer for the BBC, was Performance Consultant for the film *Shakespeare in Love* and was awarded a David Fraser/Andrea Wonfor Directing for Television Bursary.

His book, *Dramatic Adventures in Rhetoric*, written with Giles Taylor, is published by Oberon Books; and *Grimm Tales* is published by Nick Hern Books.

MATTHEW WRIGHT
Designer

Matthew's award winning designs include *La Cage Aux Folles*, originally for Menier Chocolate Factory and subsequently for the West End, Broadway and US tour. He received Drama Desk and Outer Critics Circle Awards for '*Outstanding Costume Design'*, and Tony and Olivier Award nominations for '*Best Costume Design'*.

Costume Design credits include: *Funny Girl, Sweet Charity* (West End/ Menier Chocolate Factory)*; What's It All About: Bacharach Re-Imagined, The Color Purple, Road Show, The Invisible Man* (Menier Chocolate Factory) and *Close To You* (West End)*.

Production Designer credits include: *The Norman Conquests, Kes* (Liverpool Playhouse); *Legally Blonde* (Leicester Curve); *Sister Act* (Tour); *Breakfast at Tiffany's* (Leicester Curve, UK Tour, West End); *White Christmas, Larkin With Women* (West Yorkshire Playhouse); *Calamity Jane* (Watermill/Tour); *Speaking Like Magpies* (RSC/West End); *Evita* (West End, UK/International Tour); *Shadowlands, The Glass Menagerie* (West End); *Richard III, Reinternment Ceremony* (Leicester Cathedral, final day); *They're Playing Our Song* (Menier); *In Praise of Love* (Chichester); *Merit, Presence, The Green Man* (also Bush Theatre), *Royal Supreme, Blood Red Saffron Yellow, Musik, The Imposter* (Plymouth Theatre Royal); *The Hired Man* (NYMT); *The Dishwashers* (Birmingham Rep/Tour); *Carnaby Street, Brother Love's Travelling Salvation Show, Clouds* (Tour); *A Man of No Importance, Stepping Out, Alphabetical Order* (Salisbury Playhouse); *A Song at Twilight* (Colchester/Tour); *The Mare Rider* (Arcola); *One Under* (Tricycle); *US and Them, The Dead Eye Boy* (Hampstead); *On The Ceiling* (West End/ Birmingham Rep); *Behzti, Getting To The Foot of The Mountain* (Birmingham Rep); *Neville's Island, A Taste of Honey, Absurd Person Singular* (Watford); *Deadeye, Bells & Chaos, Paper Thin* (Kali) and *Arcadia* (Northampton).

ALEX SMITH
Arranger & Musical Director

Alex trained at The Liverpool Institute for Performing Arts and graduated in 2010. As well as working as a musical director Alex is a trumpet player with British military band; *The Band of The Duke of Lancaster's Regiment*. The band performs music at many high-profile, ceremonial military events in the North West and represents the UK on tours across the world.

Theatre credits include: *Shout! The Mod Musical, Pharaoh 'Cross the Mersey, Mam I'm 'Ere, Scouse of the Antarctic, A Hitchhikers guide to Fazakerley* (Royal Court, Liverpool); *Our Day Out* (Oldham Coliseum); *Betty Blue Eyes* (Cameron Mackintosh UK tour); *West Side Story* (Liverpool Empire); *Mam I'm 'Ere* (The Dome Liverpool); *Sweet Charity* and *A Chorus Line* (LIPA).

JOHANNA TOWN
Lighting Designer

Johanna is an Associate Artist for Theatre 503 and an Honorary Fellow at Guildhall School of Music and Drama.

Theatre credits include:*The Norman Conquests, Brassed Off, Popcorn, Les Liason Dangereuses, The Playboy of the Western World, Shadow of a Gunman* (Liverpool Playhouse); *Orca* (Southwark); *Fracked!* (Chichester); *Here I Belong* (Pentabus); *The Tempest* (Northampton/NYT); *My Mother Said I Never Should* (St James); *King Lear* (Talawa/ Royal Exchange, Manchester/Birmingham Rep); *Brainstorm* (National); *Five Finger Exercise* (Print Room); *The Nap* (Sheffield) *and Don Quixote* (RSC). *Dear Lupin, Fences, What the Butler Saw, Some Like It Hip Hop, Betrayal, Speaking in Tongues, Beautiful Thing* (West End); *Rose* (National/Broadway); *My Name is Rachel Corrie* (Royal Court/West End/ NY); *Guantanamo* (NY/Tricycle/West End); *Arabian Nights, Our Lady of Sligo* (NY); *Haunted* (Royal Exchange/NY/Sydney Opera House) *The Steward of Christendom* (Out Of Joint/ Broadway/ Sydney); *Macbeth* (Out Of Joint/World Tour) *The Permanent Way* (Out Of Joint/ National/ Sydney) *Our Country's Good* (Out Of Joint/ Toronto/ USA); *Porgy & Bess* (Royal Danish Opera), *Rinaldo* (Estonian National Opera); *Carmen* and *Kátya Kabanová* (Scottish Opera).

JOHN LEONARD
Sound Designer

John started work in theatre sound over 40 years ago and during that time he has provided soundtracks for theatres all over the world. Author of an acclaimed guide to theatre sound, he is the recipient of multiple awards, a Fellow of The Guildhall School of Music & Drama and an Honorary Fellow of The Hong Kong Academy of Performing Arts.

Recent sound designs include: *Dead Funny* (West-End); *One Night In Miami* (Donmar); *The Libertine* (Bath Theatre Royal and West-End); *Macbeth* (Shakespeare's Globe); *Long Day's Journey Into Night* (Bristol Old Vic); *Lawrence After Arabia, Ken* (Hampstead Theatre); *Firebird* (Hampstead Theatre & Trafalgar Studios); *Hand To God* (West End); *Into The Woods* (Royal Exchange, Manchester); *Little Eyolf* (Almeida), *Waste* (National Theatre); *Mr. Foote's Other Leg*, (Hampstead Theatre & West-End); *Just Jim Dale* (West End), *McQueen* (St. James Theatre & West-End); *Pig Farm* (St. James Theatre); *Ghosts* (Almeida/West End/New York); *Luna Gale, Matchbox Theatre, Stevie, Farewell To The Theatre* (Hampstead); *Red Dragon, White Dragon* (Cumberland Lodge, Windsor Great Park) *The BFG* (Birmingham Rep); *84 Charing Cross Road, Separate Tables, Bedroom Farce* (Salisbury Playhouse); *A View From the Bridge* (Liverpool Playhouse & UK Tour); *Moon Tiger* (Theatre Royal Bath/UK tour); *The Duck House* (West End/tour); *A Little Hotel on the Side* (Theatre Royal Bath) and *Quartermaine's Terms* (West End).

Other theatre work includes: *Untold Stories - Cocktail Sticks* (National Theatre/ West End); *Bully Boy* (St. James); *Birthday and Tribes* (Royal Court); *Ladies in Lavender* (Northampton/tour); *The Heresy of Love* (RSC); *Rattigan's Nijinsky* and *The Deep Blue Sea* (Chichester Festival Theatre); *The Master Builder*, *The Dark Earth* and *The Light Sky* and *Becky Shaw* (Almeida); *The Silver Tassie* (Druid - Galway/tour/New York); *Grief, Detroit, 2000 Years, England People Very Nice, The Power Of Yes, Paul, London Assurance* and *Much Ado About Nothing* (National Theatre).

CRESSIDA CARRÉ
Choreographer

**Choreographic and Musical Staging credits
include:** *Sweeney Todd* (Derby Theatre &
Colchester Mercury); *Eurobeat* (Edinburgh
2016); *Titanic* (Charing Cross Theatre 2016);
Laila the Musical (Watford Palace Theatre/
UK Tour); *Beyond The Fence* (Sky Arts &
Arts Theatre); *Rumpelstiltskin* (MAC Belfast
& The Egg, Bath); *Grand Tour* (Finborough
Theatre); *Titanic* (Southwark Playhouse &
Princess of Wales Theatre, Toronto); *Avenue Q*
(Greenwich Theatre & UK Tour); *The Jungle
Book* (Citizens Theatre, Glasgow); *Sweeney
Todd* (Centrepoint Theatre, Dubai); *Spend
Spend Spend* (Cockpit Theatre); *Seussical*
(Arts Theatre); *A Winter's Tale* (Landor
Theatre); *Marguerite* (Tabard); *CATS* (Dubai);
Bright Lights Big City (Albany Theatre);
Songs Of My Life (Garrick Theatre); *The Lost
Christmas* (Waterloo East Theatre); *Burlesque*
(Jermyn St Theatre); *Britain's Got Bhangra*
(Watford Palace & UK Tour); *FRESHER:The
Musical* (Edinburgh Festival); *The Hired Man*
(Landor Theatre); *As You Like It* and *Merlin
& The Woods Of Time* (both Grosvenor Park
Open Air Theatre); *Spring Awakening* (UK
Tour); *The Great British Musical* (Criterion
Theatre); *Great Expectations* (Watford Palace
& UK tour); *Cinderella* (Devonshire Park,
Eastbourne); *Wind In The Willows* (Derby
LIVE); *Departure Lounge* (Waterloo East
Theatre*); Elegies For Angels Punks And Raging
Queens* (The Black Box, Belfast); *A Chorus
Line* (BAC); *Departure Lounge* (Edinburgh
Festival); *Into The Woods* (Greenwich Theatre),
Jack And The Beanstalk (Theatre Royal, Bury
St Edmunds); *Witches Of Eastwick* (Albany
Theatre); *Blues Brothers* (Centrepoint Theatre,
Dubai); *Hot Mikado* (Chelsea Theatre); *Peter
Pan* (Millfield Theatre) and *Lucky Stiff* (New
Wimbledon Studio).

Directing credits include: *Eurobeat*
(Edinburgh 2016); *Avenue Q* (Greenwich
Theatre & UK Tour), *Spear* (Courtyard Theatre,
Hereford), *The Lost Christmas* (Trafalgar
Studios), *Betwixt* (Edinburgh Festival) and
Marry Me A Little (Etcetera Theatre).

Awards include: Off West End Awards for
Best Choreography & What's On Stage Award
for Best Off West End Production for *Titanic*
(Southwark Playhouse).

JOHN BULLEID
Magic Consultant

John is an actor, magician and theatre
consultant. He has been the face of an
advertising campaign for Deloitte and in 2015
was elevated to the level of Associate of the
Inner Magic Circle with Silver Star.

Theatre credits include: *The Gypsy Thread*
(National Theatre Studio); *The Inn At Lydda*
(Shakespeare's Globe); *Partners In Crime*
(Queen's Theatre Hornchurch); *Dirty Dancing*
(Secret Cinema); *Dracula* (Paul Ewing
Entertainment, Thailand); *The Ladykillers,
The Secret Adversary* (Watermill Theatre);
Thark (Park Theatre); *Alice In Wonderland*
(Brewhouse Theatre, Taunton); *Murder Most
Fowl* (Quay Arts Centre) and *A Midsummer
Night's Dream* (Theatre in the Forest).

Television and film credits include: *'Coco'
Rep*ort (Channel 4 News) and *You And
Universe, Loo* (Independent Short Films).

JACK COOPER
Assistant Director

Jack graduated Liverpool John Moores
University with a degree in Drama and English
Literature. Following graduation, he became a
YEP Young Director at the Liverpool Everyman
& Playhouse. He has worked extensively with
the Liverpool Expressive Arts Forum to create
theatre with local schools and communities, and
is the recipient of the Andrew Lloyd-Webber
Foundation Award for Young Directors.

Director credits include: *Trojan Women* (The
Blade Factory); *Hot Mess* (The Everyman
Young Directors' Festival) *and Frankenstein*
(The Dome Theatre, Liverpool).

Assistant Director credits include:
The Bells (Hazard Theatre) *and The
Radicalisation of Bradley Manning* (Young
Everyman Playhouse).

The Star is Jack's first professional credit.

For the Everyman & Playhouse

The Star

Michael Wynne was born and brought up in Birkenhead. His first play *The Knocky* (Meyer Whitworth Award – Best New Playwright and Best New Writer Nomination – Writers' Guild) was produced by the Royal Court. His other credits for the Royal Court include *Who Cares, The Priory* (Olivier Award – Best New Comedy), *The People Are Friendly, The Red Flag* and *Friday Night Sex*. Wynne's work also includes the first new play at the rebuilt Liverpool Everyman, *Hope Place*, and *Canvas* (Minerva Theatre, Chichester), *Sell Out* (Best Off West End – *Time Out* Theatre Awards) and *Dirty Wonderland* (both Frantic Assembly), *Tits/Teeth* (Soho Theatre) and *The Boy Who Left Home* (Actors Touring Company). He has also written extensively for screen, including *My Summer of Love* (BAFTA – Best British Film, *Evening Standard* Film Awards; Best Screenplay, The Michael Powell Award for Best British Film at the Edinburgh Film Festival; joint winner of the Directors' Guild Award for Best British Film), *Lapland* and *Being Eileen* for the BBC.

MICHAEL WYNNE

The Star

FABER & FABER

First published in 2016

by Faber and Faber Limited
74–77 Great Russell Street, London WC1B 3DA

Typeset by Country Setting, Kingsdown, Kent CT14 8ES
Printed in England by CPI Group (UK) Ltd, Croydon CR0 4YY

A CIP record for this book is available from the British Library

ISBN 978-0-571-33739-2

2 4 6 8 10 9 7 5 3 1

For my sisters
Helen and Rachel

The Star was first produced at the Liverpool Playhouse on 9 December 2016. The cast, in alphabetical order, was as follows:

Ellen Eithne Browne
Ida Michelle Butterly
Dora Helen Carter
Mr Charles Kevin Harvey
Arthur Crown Danny O'Brien
Jack Jack Rigby
The Chairman Michael Starke

Other parts played by members of the company

*Musician*s James Breckon, Elliot Chapman, Danny Miller

Director Philip Wilson
Designer Matthew Wright
Arranger and Musical Director Alex Smith
Lighting Designer Johanna Town
Sound Designer John Leonard
Choreographer Cressida Carré
Magic Consultant John Bulleid
Assistant Director Jack Cooper
Casting Consultant Kay Magson CDG

This version of the text went to print
before the end of rehearsals and may
differ slightly from the version performed.

Characters

The Chairman

Dame Ellen

Arthur Crown

Dora

Jack

Ida Valentine

Mr Charles

*Other characters played
by members of the company*

Songs

THE STAR

Act One

Possible overture as audience take their seats – just quite simple on the piano.

A beautiful music-hall stage. Lavish red curtains and various backdrops that change according to the song. A golden glow from footlights along the front, orchestra pit below.

Sharp blackout. Music starts – only honky-tonk piano at first. Ellen appears in a tight spotlight, her face peeking round the corner of the scenery. She's a Florrie Forde type character, dressing regally in pearls and a large hat.

She sings the first chorus in the spotlight just accompanied by the Musical Director on the piano.

DON'T DILLY-DALLY

Ellen

We had to move away,
Cos the rent we couldn't pay
The moving van came round just after dark
There was me and my old man
Shoving things inside the van
Which we'd often done before let me remark
We packed all that could be packed
In the van, and that's a fact
And we got inside all we could get inside
Then we packed all we could pack
On the tail board at the back
Till there wasn't any room for me to ride.

Ellen bursts out from behind the flat as the stage is bathed in golden light – with her in a follow spot. The full band now joins in.

Ellen You all know this.

Chorus.
My old man said follow the van
And don't dilly-dally on the way
Off went the cart with the home packed in it
I walked behind with me old cock linnet
But I dillied and dallied
Dallied and dillied
Lost the van and don't know where to roam
You can't trust these specials like the old time coppers
When you can't find your way home.

'Don't Dilly-Dally' continues to play underneath.
Ellen dances off one side of the stage.
The Chairman appears. He has a large gavel in his
hand – which he bangs against anything nearby to
keep the audience under control. He runs the theatre –
introducing the acts and keeping the audience in
check. He'll pop up all around the theatre – in the
circle, orchestra pit, stalls, flies – never in the same
place twice.

The Chairman Welcome, welcome, welcome to the Star
Music Hall, Liverpool.

What better way to start than a song about not paying
your rent and doing a runner in the middle of the night!

I'm your chairman. This is my gaff and you're all very
welcome. Are you happy to be here?

Mixed response.

No? Yes? Some of you are. Do you mind letting your
faces know?

There's hundreds of music halls all over Liverpool. The
Tivoli, Dingle Park Palace, Prince of Wales, Empire, Lyric
in Everton Valley. The Floral Pavilion and Argyle over the
water in Birkenhead. But The Star is the best by far.

Have we got a night of magic and wonderment for you. (*To Musical Director.*) Have we?

The Musical Director in the pit shrugs.

Maybe not. Let's see more of our first act, the old mother of our Music Hall . . .

Ellen pokes her head round the scenery.

Ellen Less of the old.

Music stops.

(*With great emotion.*) This will probably be my last performance.

The Chairman She's been saying that for thirty years.

Music starts again.

She's so old, when she went to school there was no history class. She's so old, she was a waitress at the Last Supper. She's so old, she's even got an autographed Bible. She's so old, she remembers when these jokes were new. The everlasting, effervescent, elderly . . . excellent, extraordinary, electric, ever ready, efflorescent, glad I've got me teeth in, entertaining, effortless, earthenware, erect, unlike you over there, sir . . .

All the way from Allerton. You've already seen her. The enchanting Dame Ellen Bloggs.

He disappears off one side of the stage.
Ellen appears and sings.

Ellen
Oh I'm in such a mess
I don't know the new address
Don't even know the blessed neighbourhood
And I feel as if I might
Have to stay out all the night
And it ain't a going to do me any good

17

I don't make no complaints
But I'm coming over faint
What I want now is a good substantial feed
And I sort o' kind o' feel
If I don't soon have a meal
I shall have to rob the linnet of its seed.

All join in now, ladies and gentlemen.

Chorus.
My old man said follow the van
And don't dilly-dally on the way
Off went the cart with the home packed in it
I walked behind with me old cock linnet
But I dillied and dallied
Dallied and dillied
Lost the van and don't know where to roam
You can't trust these specials like the old time coppers
When you can't find your way home.

*The Chairman appears round the other side of the
stage – huffing and puffing. Ellen disappears for a
moment.*

The Chairman I'm out of breath already and we're only
on page two.

*Intro to 'Down at the Old Bull and Bush' plays
underneath.*

*Jack, the young stagehand, is planted in the
audience. He wears a hat and scarf to look like a street
urchin.*

Ah, young urchin, who I've never met before. May I ask
why you like coming to the Star Music Hall?

Jack / Urchin (*read out in a very cod way*) 'Life for the
working classes these days is wretched. The music hall
provides the only escape from the grim reality that is my
existence.'

18

The Chairman That is fascinating that is.

Jack / Urchin Did I do it all right?

The Chairman Perfect. That's the educational bit over. We should still get our Arts Council grant now.

Jack / Urchin So you can pay me now?

The Chairman Maybe.

Jack dashes off.

Let's crack on and enjoy ourselves, 'Down at the Old Bull and Bush'.

Ellen reappears with the rest of company in a production number. They are in an old pub and have tankards in their hands.

DOWN AT THE OLD BULL AND BUSH

Ellen and company sing two choruses and a verse of 'Down at the Old Bull and Bush'.
  The Chairman reappears.

The Chairman Let's hear it for Dame Ellen Bloggs of Allerton.

Ellen bows and saunters off.

Isn't she wonderful? We've got lots of other exciting acts tonight. Boris, the human cannon ball. Oh yes. And a real treat. Dr Colon and his magical large intestine. Less said about that the better. One act I know you're all dying to see. (*He whispers offstage.*) Has she turned up yet?

Jack (*now at side of the stage*) Still no sign of her.

The Chairman (*aside*) I knew it was a mistake. (*Back out front.*) And now, if you want a real good laugh . . . (*Under his breath.*) You might want to go somewhere else.

No, no. It's your favourite act . . . Mr Comedy himself. Yes, it's the mirth-making, side-splitting, some say suicide-inducing Arthur Crown. Eh and no throwing rotten vegetables until I've left the stage this time.

Arthur comes on with a coal scuttle and a large fish under his arm.

Arthur Has anyone seen my coal scuttle?

Tumbleweed moment. He looks at the fish under his arm.

This fish you say, madam? I caught it this morning. I called it cold. I caught a cold.

Tumbleweed.

My wife. I wouldn't say she was fat but she wears big clothes.

Tumbleweed. He's getting desperate, he tries his catch phrase again.

Has anyone seen my coal scuttle?

Groans from the audience.

SCENE TWO

We go backstage. We are simply the other side of the backdrop.
We can see Arthur's silhouette as he performs on stage.
There's a real sense of the show going on in the background whenever we are backstage.
There's much activity and busy-ness as they try to get the show on – props, costumes, sets wheeled on and off in the background, different acts passing by, Jack and Dora continually running about.
All quite frenetic.

The Chairman and Ellen listen to Arthur's act.

The Chairman He's dying on his arse.

Ellen Again.

Audience Member Boo.

Audience Member Get him off.

Audience Member Someone shoot him.

The Chairman They're getting violent.

Ellen Again.

Arthur (*desperate, off*) Has anyone seen my coal scuttle?

The Chairman Where the hell is she?

Dora, the wig girl, is busy pushing a rail of costumes through.

Ellen I told you it was a mistake asking her back.

The Chairman (*in a panic*) What acts have we got to go on instead? Is that Bear in a Dress still about?

Ida Valentine sweeps in – she wears a large fur coat and hat and carries lots of bags and hat boxes. All the frenetic activity backstage freezes – a dramatic entrance. She's very grand and speaks in a silky, smoky theatrical voice, which disappears and becomes broadest Scouse when she's angry or upset.

Ida I'm here now, duckie.

The Chairman You're late, Ida Valentine, you were meant to perform tonight.

Ida There's still plenty of time for that.

She stands there with all her boxes and hat boxes trying to look dignified but starting to struggle under the weight. One hat box falls, then another . . .

(*In Scouse.*) Is anyone gonna help me or wha'?

Dora runs up to assist. Ida dumps everything on her.

Ellen (*aside*) You can take the girl out of New Brighton –

Ida sees Ellen.

Ida Darling. You're still here.

Ellen Where else would I be?

Ida The undertakers?

The Chairman Ellen's part of the furniture.

Ida Hmm, like a burst sofa.

A furious Ellen moves to confront her. The Chairman holds her back.

Ellen Don't you come back here now, lady . . .

Ida Now where's my dressing room?

Dora This way, Madame . . . Lady . . . Miss Valentine.

Ida (*directed at Ellen*) I take it it's the Number One Dressing Room?

Dora shows Ida to her dressing room – struggling with the boxes and dropping a few on the way. Ida picks them up as she goes – trying to look elegant in her exit but thwarted.

For crying out loud.

Ellen Why has she got star billing and the Number One Dressing Room? I thought I was the star.

The Chairman The building is The Star, that's what it's called.

Ellen Don't play silly beggars with me. Why's she back?

The Chairman The audience love her.

Ellen And what about me?

The Chairman You're always telling me it's your last ever performance, I'm covering me back.

Ellen I'm not dead yet.

The Chairman (*aside*) Don't I know it. (*To Ellen.*) You're the heart of this place, you'll always be here.

Ellen And what about this Alfonso chap she ran off with?

The Chairman Don't mention his name!

His leg and head twitches at hearing his name. He gets them under control.

Ellen Is it because you still love her?

The Chairman No. No, no, no, no, no. God, no.

Much booing and jeering from the stage. Arthur comes backstage covered in all sorts of vegetables. The band plays a jaunty tune to cover his exit.

Arthur Who knew a whole cabbage thrown at your head could hurt so much?

The Chairman I did see someone filling a cauliflower with lead shot earlier.

Ellen Bit of chicken stock, you could make a nice pan of soup with all that.

Arthur I do prefer the rotten ones. Softer. Where are they getting all these vegetables from?

The Chairman I really don't know. It's awful, awful . . .

Arthur I'm determined to find an act they love.

He leaves on one side. Jack appears on the other with a tray on a neck strap full of vegetables and a sign saying VEG TO THROW AT UNFUNNY COMIC 2/6d.

Ellen That's terrible.

The Chairman I've got to make me money somehow.

A large sinister 'swell'-type character, Mr Charles, dressed in a black cape and top hat and carrying an open bottle of champagne, appears in the shadows. Perhaps he's been standing there the whole time but in amongst props and costumes. It's only when he moves that we see him. Or he always appears by some magical trick – not quite in a puff of smoke but via a trapdoor . . .

Mr Charles You can't see me. Boo.

SCENE THREE

Number One Dressing Room.
Mirror with lights, dressing table, screens, some simple flowers.
Ida is taking in the room with a sense of drama. Dora buzzes around her – though she's quite clumsy.

Ida Here it is. This is where it started. Where all the magic began.

Dora Do you do magic as well? Can you pull a rabbit from a hat? I'd love that.

Ida No, no, duckie. (*She breathes it in.*) Can you feel the magic here?

Dora Where? Is someone doing tricks?

Ida The memories. The ghosts.

Dora Don't tell me it's haunted in 'ere.

Ida It . . . doesn't . . . matter.

Ida starts to get ready for the show.

24

Dora Is there anything I can get you Mrs, Miss Valentine? A drink.

Ida A glass of water. Maybe put some gin in it.

Dora Okay, Miss.

Dora curtsies awkwardly and rushes out as the Chairman enters. Ida is busy getting ready, she's almost dismissive at first.

The Chairman There you are. It is good to see you.

Ida I'm sure it is.

The Chairman You haven't changed.

Ida goes behind a screen. We can just see her head as she gets changed.

Ida Can't remember the last time I saw you.

The Chairman I can. (*Slight twitch.*) Maybe the less said about that the better.

Ida It's freezing here though. I do miss the warmth. I did love the sun in – sorry, I shouldn't mention – you know, Spain.

The Chairman It's fine . . . (*Twitch of the head.*) Doesn't bother me . . . (*Twitch of leg.*) Spain.

Ida Really?

The Chairman All in the past. Eh, how many Spaniards does it take to change a lantern?

She doesn't really engage.

Ida I really don't know.

The Chairman Just Juan!

Ida Where's that drink?

Dora (*off*) Coming now.

A glass smashes, off.

(*Off.*) Oops. I'll get you another one.

The Chairman What were the two Spanish firemen called? Hose A and Hose B.

Ida Okay, I can see you're fine about it. So my first song –

The Chairman What about the Spanish streaker? Senor Willy.

Ida You're overcompensating now. And I wasn't going to even mention Alfonso.

The Chairman Alfonso . . . (*Leg twitch.*) I have no problem with him. Is he here? Love to see his shiny round Spanish face.

Ida (*shouting, off*) Where's that drink?

Dora (*off*) Coming.

Glass smashes.

Oops.

Ida Where did you find her? (*In Scouse.*) I'll get one meself.

She heads out.

The Chairman (*under his breath*) Why did I invite her back? (*Raging.*) Alfonso!

He starts twitching all over. The intro starts.

I can remember it all now. Where it all went wrong.

He sings.

The Chairman

    List to me while I tell you of
    The Spaniard that blighted my life
    List to me while I tell you of
    The man that pinched my future wife
    'Twas at the bullfight that we met him
    We'd been watching his daring display
    And while I'd gone out for some nuts and a programme
    The dirty dog stole her away, oh yes, oh yes
    But I've sworn to have my revenge.

*He makes a cape and red flag out of bits of costume
left about.*

Chorus.

    If I catch Alphonso Spagoni the toreador
    With a mighty swipe I will dislocate his bally jaw
    I'll fight the bullfighter I will
    And when I catch the bounder, the blighter I'll kill
    He shall die, he shall die
    He shall die tid-dly-i ti-ti-ti-ti-ti-ti
    He shall die, he shall die
    For I'll raise a bunion on his Spanish onion
    If I catch him bending tonight.

    Yes, when I catch Spagoni he will wish that he'd
        never been born
    And for this special reason my stiletto I've fetched out
        of pawn
    It cost me five shillings to fetch it
    This expense it has caused me much pain
    But the pawnbroker's promised when I've killed Spagoni
    He'll take it in pawn once again, oh yes, oh yes
    So tonight there will be dirty work.

Chorus.

    If I catch Alphonso Spagoni the toreador

27

With a mighty swipe I will dislocate his bally jaw
I'll fight the bullfighter I will (he will)
And when I catch the bounder, the blighter I'll kill
He shall die (he shall die), he shall die (I'll kill him)
He shall die tiddly-i-ti ti-ti-ti-ti-ti
He shall die, he shall die
For I'll raise a bunion on his Spanish onion
If I catch him bending tonight.

Olé!

SCENE FOUR

*On stage, the band strikes up with some dark mysterious
music and spotlights search the stage. Arthur steps out all
dressed in black with a blindfold on and a large white 'R'
on his chest. He steps forward in a sharp pool of light –
confidently at first . . .*

The Chairman (*voice from off*) Let's hear it for the man
of mystery, mischief and memory, Dr Recall.

*Arthur loses confidence in his walk and starts grabbing
about in the dark, as he can't see where he's going. He
turns round in a circle and ends up facing upstage, his
back to the audience. He stands with confidence,
hands on hips in a sharp pool of light. The Chairman
comes on.*

What are we dealing with here? (*Aside.*) Yeah, it's Arthur
Crown, trying out a new act.

He turns Arthur round to face the audience.

Dr Recall will astound you with his feats of mind-reading
and memory. Never seen before on this stage . . . (*Aside.*)
And probably never seen again. I give you Dr Recall, the
memory man.

Arthur stands still, deep in concentration. The
Chairman waits for something to happen. Nothing does.

Arthur Am I right, sir?

The Chairman Sorry, ladies and gentlemen. (*to Arthur*)
We're not at that bit yet, are we? What happens now?

Arthur Am I right, sir? (*Muffled.*) I've forgotten. Can't
remember.

The Chairman Dr Recall, the memory man who can't
remember his act?! Get off.

He pushes Arthur off into the wings.

How we doing? Still with us?
    There's a couple of rowdy ones over here. Up in the
cheap seats.
    You lot in from Kirkby? Is that your charabang
outside? You've got all those lovely fields and countryside
in Kirkby. Let's hope they never build on it.
    Where else have you come from tonight?
    Anyone from The Wirral? Come across in your boats?
Of course, sitting down here in the dear seats. They think
they're posh. They're so posh that they get out of the
bath to pee.
    You ready for the next act? I don't know whether I
am. (*To himself.*) What have I done? Yes, she's back to
her first love . . . Not me, I didn't mean me . . .

Audience Member Get on with it.

The Chairman Well said, sir . . . Her first love, The Star
music hall – where she made her name.
    As part of her world tour, fresh from Sp— (*He can't
quite say it – he spits it out.*) Spain. Performing one of her
classics. All about New Brighton Promenade. Glamorous,
ain't it?
    The irrepressible, imitable, indisputable, irritating,
infuriating, impossible, intolerable, Miss Ida Valentine!

Ida sweeps out to perform.

Ida I'm back. My stage. My people. You ready,
Liverpool?

She sings.

WHEN I TAKE MY MORNING PROMENADE

Ida
Since Mother Eve in the garden long ago
Started the fashion, fashion's been the passion
She wore a strip that has mystified the priests
Still every season brought a change of green
She'd stare if she came to town
What would Mother Eve think of my new Parisian
     gown?

Chorus.
As I take my morning promenade
Quite a fashion card, on the promenade
Now I don't mind nice boys staring hard
If it satisfies their desire
Do you think that my dress is a little bit
Just a little bit – not too much of it?
If it shows my shape just a little bit
That's the little bit the boys admire.

You need livening up. How about a little song about a
vegetable?

She sings.

OH WHAT A BEAUTY! (THE MARROW SONG)

*Ida sings two verses and two choruses of the Marrow
Song, 'Oh What a Beauty'.*

*We go backstage – the show continues out front. We hear
the Chairman on stage.*

*Dora and Jack are busy running about moving scenery
and props. We catch glimpses of strange and wonderful
acts as they prepare to go on.*

The Chairman (*off*) Who knew a green vegetable could
be so entertaining? (*Aside.*) Maybe she is worth the grief.
Miss Ida Valentine! The thrills and spills keep coming.
What's next? He loves getting his knickers in a twist. It's
time for Colin the Contortionist.

*'Oohs' and 'Aahs' from the audience as Colin starts
bending and stretching. Ida passes through from the
stage.*

Ida I love that stage. I've still got it.

Ellen (*under her breath*) Yes, you've still got something,
my dear. Did you catch it off Alfonso? You might want to
pop down the clinic.

Ida (*aside, as she passes, all smiles*) Cow.

Ellen (*aside, as she passes, all smiles*) Tramp.

*The Chairman comes backstage, busy dashing about.
Arthur passes through. Groans from the audience at
Colin's act.*

The Chairman Ow, Colin, I don't know how he got his
head up there. Who we got on next?

Ida (*to The Chairman*) Duckie, I feel alive.

The Chairman You were amazing.

Ida I'm so glad you invited me back.

The Chairman (*distracted*) I'm made up.

Ida That rapport with my people, the feeling of us together as one made me think fondly of me and you and how it all started here . . .

The Chairman is looking round, wanting to get the next act ready.

Ida (*in Scouse*) Am I boring you?

The Chairman No, it's wonderful. But I've got a show to put on here.

Ida Ah, of course, The Star always comes first with you.

She storms off to her dressing room. Jack dashes on.

Jack Very important-looking letter for you, Chairman.

Arthur passes through.

The Chairman (*cod voice*) I should open it now, as it might contain an important part of the plot. (*He opens it, scans it very quickly.*) Shock. It says we've got a new owner.

Arthur Who is it?

The Chairman It doesn't say.

Arthur What are their plans?

The Chairman It doesn't say.

Arthur Not much of a letter.

The Chairman You don't say.

Jack moves a large piece of scenery and Mr Charles is revealed in his top hat and tails. He's sitting behind it on a bicycle – with his open bottle of champagne.

Ellen (*to Arthur*) Who is that strange mysterious character?

Mr Charles Oh, you can see me?

The Chairman Quite hard to miss, mate.

Arthur He's dead sinister, him. Gives me the willies.

Mr Charles Me, sinister? It's all this garb. And maybe my maniacal laugh. (*He laughs a long laugh.*) Ooh ha ha ha haaaaa.

Ellen Yeah, that's quite sinister, that.

Mr Charles I suppose it is.

He cycles off.

Ellen He seems very posh and sophisticated. Like me.

Arthur Who *is* he?

Ellen Frigged if I know. But I imagine he's quite central to the plot, so hopefully we'll find out soon.

The Chairman Hang on. We've got a new owner and there's this strange mysterious character lurking about. I wonder if the two are connected?

They all think.

Ellen Hmm.

Arthur Naah.

The Chairman Didn't think so. Back to work.

They all get back to putting on the show.
Instrumental of 'Are We to Part Like This, Bill?' as we change scenes.

SCENE SIX

Number One Dressing Room.
Ida is having her hair done by Dora, who is fussing and flustered around Ida.

Ida Ow, careful with your pins, my dear. You're meant to be putting my wig on, not practising acupuncture.

33

Dora Sorry, Miss Valentine.

Ida Now I want you to – Ow. You've stabbed me again.

Dora I'm sorry, Miss. I'm all fingers and thumbs.

Ida What is wrong with you?

Dora Nothing. I'm fine . . . (*She starts crying but tries to cover it.*) Fii . . . iiine.

Ida What's that snivelling noise? Is it you?

Dora No, no, Miss Valentine.

She cries some more, much louder.

Ida Well, there's someone crying in this room and it's not me. I wonder who it is.

Dora I can't think who it could be.

Ida (*impatient*) Oh, what is wrong?

Dora It's Bill. We've split up and I can't think straight and . . .

She continues to explain but cries as she does, so it's indecipherable.

I saw him the other night and he was with an old pal of mine and . . .

Ida Didn't understand a word of that.

Dora (*crying through it – indecipherable*) I thought there was still a chance that we'd . . . But now it looks like we'll never be together ever . . .

Ida Take a deep breath, duckie.

Dora breathes and calms herself down.

Why don't you tell me all about it through the medium of song.

Dora You wha'?

Ida Sing it. Your turn for a song.

Dora Oh, okay.

She sings – Ida listens.

ARE WE TO PART LIKE THIS, BILL?

Dora
Three weeks ago, no longer
I was as gay as a bird on the wing
But since me and Bill have been parted, you know
Life is a blank and it's changed everything
I saw him out with another last night
None can guess how I felt at the sight
With tears in my eyes that I tried to keep back
I crept to his side and said . . .

Chorus.
Are we to part like this, Bill
Are we to part this way?
Who's it to be, 'er or me?
Don't be afraid to say
If everything's over between us
Don't never pass me by
Cos you and me still friends can be
For the sake of the days gone by.

We went to school together
Lived side by side, me and Bill, in the mews
When 'e was ill, too, I stayed up for nights
Nursed him – to do it I'd never refuse
'E used to tell me his wife I should be
I never thought that he'd turn against me
Sleeping or waking, at work or at home
I find myself murmuring this,

Chorus.
>Are we to part like this, Bill
>Are we to part this way?
>Who's it to be, 'er or me?
>Don't be afraid to say
>If everything's over between us
>Don't never pass me by
>Cos you and me still friends can be
>For the sake of the days gone by.

Jack enters behind to give Ida her call. He stops and listens. He's clearly in love with Dora.

Dora
>Down in a little laundry
>Me and 'er worked side by side every day
>She was my pal and I looked to 'er well
>Trusted and helped 'er in every way
>Still if my Bill cares more for 'er than me
>I wish 'm no harm no, but prosperity
>I try to forget him, but each day I find
>These words running through my mind.

Chorus.
>Are we to part like this, Bill
>Are we to part this way?
>Who's it to be, 'er or me?
>Don't be afraid to say
>If everything's over between us
>Don't never pass me by
>Cos you and me still friends can be
>For the sake of the days gone by.

Ida holds her hand. Jack is still watching; he almost reaches out to her, wanting to comfort and hold her.

Ida Oh my dear. Come here. You're better off without him. There's another man out there for you.

Dora Do you think so?

Ida I know there is.

Dora What's his name?

Ida When I say I know, I don't know who it will actually . . .

Jack steps forward.

Jack This is your five-minute call.

Ida What about this handsome young lad? He'd be perfect.

Jack looks at her – rabbit in the footlights.

Dora Jack?

Jack (*high-pitched*) Me? Ha!

Dora Don't be silly.

Jack Crazy. Stupid, mad, maddest thing I've ever heard of. Who'd think that? Us two, me and her, her and me . . .

Ida Have you quite finished?

Jack Yeah. Five-minute call. Well, four minutes now.

He rushes off.

Dora If only there was someone round here who loved me.

Ida (*aside*) I'm gonna have me work cut out with this one.

Dora goes back to fixing Ida's wig.

Ow!

We transition to backstage. A hint of 'Champagne Charlie' as we do.

SCENE SEVEN

Backstage. Much activity as the show goes on. Jack leading through an animal act. Arthur waddles backstage to loud boos – he's all chained and padlocked up like an escape act. He's escorted by the Chairman.

The Chairman How much had you practised?

Arthur I hadn't. I thought it'd be easy. I thought they'd love it.

The Chairman Maybe if you'd actually escaped. Who's got the keys?

Arthur I swallowed them.

Ellen You're gonna be padlocked for a while until you see *them* again.

The Chairman You might want to have a word with Dr Colon.

Mr Charles appears with a large bottle of champagne and glass.

Ellen Oh look, it's that mysterious character again.

Mr Charles Isn't this a wonderful show? The roar of the greasepaint and the smell of the crowd. I love the theatre.

Arthur Who the hell is he?

Mr Charles Champagne.

He pours himself another glass.

The Chairman Eh, mate, who are you? Who let you back here?

Mr Charles I'm a very close friend of the new owner and he said he'd let me look around this establishment.

The Chairman Who is this new owner?

Arthur Nobody's seen him.

Ellen Knows anything about him.

The Chairman Or knows what his plans are.

Mr Charles It's very mysterious, isn't it?

Ellen Quite unsettling.

Arthur It's giving me the creeps.

The Chairman Can you tell us anything?

Mr Charles I can tell you this.

They all look to him. Long pause.

I think it's time for champagne.

Arthur What's the occasion?

Mr Charles looks round for something. Nothing much to inspire. He looks at his pocket watch.

Mr Charles It's . . . It's seven fifty-two. Let's celebrate seven fifty-two. Wonderful time. And you see I like to drink champagne all day and all night.

Ellen Oh, I get it. You're an alcoholic.

Mr Charles You could put it like that.

He passes round glasses of champagne. Arthur struggles to drink all tied up.

Ellen Don't mind if I do. This will probably be my last drink.

He sings.

Mr Charles Maestro, please.

Music starts.

Mr Charles
I've seen a deal of gaiety throughout my noisy life
With all my grand accomplishments I never could get
a wife
The thing I most excel in is the PRFG game
A noise at night, in bed all day, and swimming in
champagne.

*He opens bottles and passes round many glasses of
champagne. They all join in.*

Chorus.
Champagne Charlie is my name
Champagne drinking is my game
Good for any game at night, my boys
Good for any game at night, my boys
For Champagne Charlie is my name
Champagne Charlie is my name
Good for any game at night, my boys
Who'll come and join me in a spree?

Jack and Dora appear and take glasses too.

Dora Where'd he get all this booze from?

Jack Who knows?

Arthur I'm happy as long as it keeps coming.

Mr Charles
The way I earned my title thro' a hobby I have got
Of never letting others pay however long the shot
Whoever drinks at my expense are treated all the same
From dukes and lords, to cabmen down, I make
them drink champagne.

Chorus.
Champagne Charlie is my name
Champagne drinking is my game

Good for any game at night, my boys
Good for any game at night, my boys
For Champagne Charlie is my name
Champagne Charlie is my name
Good for any game at night, my boys
Who'll come and join me in a spree?

The Chairman Eh, I don't want everyone pilatic. We've got a show to put on.

Dora I love him.

Arthur He's not that mysterious and sinister after all. He's just an old pisshead.

Music stops.

Mr Charles (*to the audience*) That's what they think.

Music starts again.

Perhaps you fancy what I say is nothing else but chaff
And only put into this song to raise a little laugh
To prove that I'm in jest each man a bottle of cham
I'll stand fizz round yes that I will and stand it like
    a lamb.
For . . .

More champagne for everyone.

Chorus.
Champagne Charlie is my name
Champagne drinking is my game
Good for any game at night, my boys
Good for any game at night, my boys
For Champagne Charlie is my name
Champagne Charlie is my name
Good for any game at night, my boys
Who'll come and join me in a spree?

I thank you. Here, eight shows a week.

The Chairman is back on stage. He bangs his hammer against the proscenium arch.

The Chairman Order, order, order. This hammer is not just for show. I'm gonna need it tonight. Especially with you lot up in the balcony. I've got your number.

He stands still a moment and holds the hammer in his hands.

Voice from Above Tonight's hammer is sponsored by Ye Olde Rapid Hardware.

The Chairman We've got to pay for this somehow.
   Now, what's next? I don't know if I'm coming or going.
   We've got Holloway, Man on a Ladder soon. Yes, that's a man standing on a ladder. Don't say we don't bring you the best acts around.

Ellen is planted in the audience as a posh woman in a big hat.

Ellen / Posh Woman I'd like to say something.

The Chairman You got round there quick. We've got an interjection by a woman in a hat. Who I've never clapped eyes on before. She's in the expensive seats. Where are you from, love?

Ellen / Posh Woman Meols. With an 'o'.

The Chairman Oh, you seem very posh . . .

Ellen / Posh Woman Well, I'm from Meols, so . . . Can I just say . . . (*Cod voice, practically reading.*) 'The Music hall is growing too popular and it's dangerous to have all these working-class people in one place. This new form of entertainment formed by the working classes for the working classes, might somehow free them from their position at the foot of the social scale. Anarchy would prevail. The workers must be kept in their place and the music halls closed down . . .'

The Chairman We don't want that, do we, ladies and gentleman? No. So sod off.

Ellen / Posh Woman Oh all right then.

She leaves.

The Chairman Ponder that while we carry on with the show. (*To a member of the audience.*) And you just thought it was gonna be a bit of 'Don't Dilly-Dally' and a sing-song didn't you? Oh aye. Let's crack on.

Intro to 'The Rest of the Day's Your Own' plays as we move backstage.

SCENE NINE

Dora sits on a large basket in a quiet corner backstage. She has some letters in her hand and is deep in thought. Jack dashes by laden with various props – including a cow's head, some vegetables from his tray earlier and milkmaid buckets.

Jack Dora! What you doing?

Dora I like it back here, it's quiet. I can get away from it all. And Ida's not on for a while.

She looks at the letters in her hands. She's not happy.

Jack Why so glum?

Dora I'm fine, it's just . . . I was re-reading some old letters from Bill.

Jack Oh, him.

43

Dora When it was going well. They're just making me sadder. I should throw them away.

Jack (*over-keen*) Yeah, rip them up into tiny teeny little pieces. So small that no one can ever read them again. Then stamp them into the ground. Or set fire to them. A huge bonfire. Do you want me to rip them up, then set fire to them for you?

Dora Not just now.

Jack I wish I could make you happy. Happier.

Dora You always cheer me up.

Jack Do I?

Dora Course. I don't think you'll have much luck today though.

Jack I do like a challenge.

The Chairman (*off*) Master Jack? Where are the hell are you?

Ellen (*off*) Jack? Darling, I need a tonic, I'm feeling so unwell . . .

Arthur (*off*) Eh, Jack? You got a hacksaw for these bloomin' chains?

Dora Where would this place be without you?

Jack Just doing me job.

Dora I love how you can do so many things at once.

Jack This is a doddle compared to the other jobs I've had. (*He looks at the cow's head and milkmaid buckets.*) Did I ever tell you when I worked on a farm?

Dora No, no.

Jack It sounds like a cue for a song.

Music starts.

Dora (*slow on the uptake*) Does it?

Jack Yeah, it is. I'm gonna sing now.

Dora Oh are y'?

Jack They've already started the intro.

Dora So they have. Ah.

Jack Maybe this will cheer you up.

Dora (*forgetting that she's sad*) Oh yeah. (*She pulls the corners of her mouth down.*) Very sad.

He looks around at the props left about. He sees a farmer's hat and some corn that he puts in his mouth.
    He sings and entertains Dora, making her laugh. She plays about with the various props he was carrying and others during the song.

THE REST OF THE DAY'S YOUR OWN

Jack
One day when I was out of work a job I went to seek
To be a farmer's boy
At last I found an easy job at half-a-crown a week
To be a farmer's boy
The farmer said, 'I think I've got the very job for you
Your duties will be light, for this is all you've got to do.'

Chorus.
Rise at three every morn,
Milk the cow with the crumpled horn
Feed the pigs, clean the sty,
Teach the pigeons the way to fly
Plough the fields, mow the hay,
Help the cocks and hens to lay
Sow the seed, tend the crops,

Chase the flies from the turnip tops
Clean the knives, black the shoes
Scrub the kitchen and sweep the flues
Help the wife, wash the pots
Grow the cabbages and carrots
Make the beds, bust the coals
Mend the gramophone
And then if there's no more work to do
The rest of the day's your own.

Dora That's amazing. You've cheered me right up.
Anyway . . .

Jack There's more.

Dora Oh go on then.

Jack
I scratched my head and thought it would be
Absolutely prime
To be a farmer's boy
The farmer said, 'You'll have to do some overtime
When you're a farmer's boy.'
Said he, 'The duties that I've given you, you'll be
quickly through
So I've been thinking of a few more things that you
can do.'

Dora He got you to do more? Cheeky get.

Jack
Skim the milk, make the cheese,
Chop the meat for the sausagees
Bath their kids, mend their clothes
Use your dial to scare the crows
In the milk put the chalk
Shave the nobs off the pickled pork
Shoe the horse, break the coal
Take the cat for his midnight stroll

46

Cook the food, scrub the stairs
Teach the parrot to say his prayers
Roast the joint, bake the bread
Shake the feathers up in the bed
When the wife's got the gout
Rub her funny bone
And if there's no more work to do
The rest of the day's your own.

Dora You must have been knackered. But glad that it was over.

Jack There's more.

Dora No? What happened?

Jack I'll tell you.

He's now becoming more manic and she's laughing much more. They both dance about to the final chorus.

I thought it was a shame to take the money, you can bet
To be a farmer's boy
And so I wrote my duties down in case I should forget
I was a farmer's boy
It took all night to write 'em down, I didn't go to bed
But somehow I got all mixed up, and this is how
    they read.

Chorus.

Rise at three, every morn
Milk the hen with a crumpled horn
Scrub the wife every day
Teach the nanny-goat how to lay
Shave the cat, mend the cheese
Fit the tights on the sausagees
Bath the pigs, break the pots
Boil the kids with a few carrots
Roast the horse, dust the bread

Put the cocks and hens to bed
Boots and shoes, black with chalk
Shave the hair on the pickled pork
All the rest I forget, somehow it had flown
But I got the sack this morning
So the rest of my life's my own.

They end up in a heap, laughing.

Dora You'd make someone a lovely boyfriend one day.

Jack Do you think?

Dora She'd be a lucky lady.

He looks at her. She looks at him. A moment between them.

Jack You know . . .

Dora (*a moment of realisation*) Why didn't I think? I can't believe I've been so stupid.

He moves closer towards her.

I'm gonna find a girl for you.

His heart sinks.

Jack I think there might be someone nearby just for me.

Dora (*oblivious*) Do y'?

She looks around – she can't see anyone.

No one round 'ere. Ellen's too old and is about to die any minute. It's not Miss Valentine, is it, cos sometimes she can be a right c—

Ida breezes in behind Jack – he doesn't see her but Dora does. She starts singing to cover what she was going to say.

(*Singing.*) 'Cover it over quick, Jemima. Cover it over quick . . .'

48

Jack What's come over you?

Dora I love that song, it's one of my favourites.

Jack now sees Ida and it makes sense – they share a laugh.

Jack I see.

Ida (*aside*) Ah the young lovers' sub-plot. How wonderful.

The Chairman (*off*) Where's Jack? It's time for the free and easies soon.

Jack scoots off.

Ida Now, darling. Some more of my luggage has apparently arrived at stage door from Espana.

Dora You wha'?

Ida From Spain. If you could bring it to the Number One Dressing Room that would be marvellous.

Dora I've never been abroad, probably never will. I wish I had your life. It's so glamorous.

Ida (*over-egging the pudding*) I know, darling. The travel. The romance. It's a constant delight.

Ellen passes. She's dressed as one of the women from 'Ride of Valkyries' – all Norse breastplate and plaits. She's not wearing the Viking helmet yet. She and Ida are all smiles.

Darling.

Ellen Sweetheart.

As Ellen walks off:

Ida (*under her breath*) Witch.

Ellen (*under her breath*) Whore.

Dora's oblivious to all this.

Dora I love it here backstage. Peeking out and watching when the show's on. I don't know where else I'd rather be.

Ida You got the bug?

Dora Oh no, just a little cough.

Ida I mean the acting, performing bug . . . Want to get out there yourself one day?

Dora I couldn't do that, what you do. Though I'd love to.

Ida Maybe you'll get your chance . . .

Dora Naaah.

Ida One day

Dora Not me.

Ida You never know.

Dora I do.

Ida I'm not gonna fight you about it.

SCENE TEN

The Chairman appears on one side of the stage in a tight spotlight. He bangs on the proscenium arch with his hammer.

The Chairman Order, order, order. You rowdy room of rambunctious rabblers. We've got another exciting act for you now. A feat of strength, muscle, brute force, brawn, very little brains . . . What's he called again? (*He looks at a piece of paper in his hand.*) I apologise for the lack of imagination, ladies and gentleman. It's Sturdy Sid the Strong Man.

Arthur appears on the other side of the stage in a spotlight. He's in a strong-man outfit of leotard, belt and sandals. He does strong-man poses, looking very serious. He then breaks character.

Arthur (*in his high-pitched friendly voice*) Hiya, it's only me, Arthur.

He goes back to being serious again.

The Chairman He's looking the part.

Arthur I've been down the gym with the big lads. Even had some of those protein potions from Ye Olde Holland and Barrett.

The Chairman See him as he bends raw steel.

Arthur has a steel bar – which is actually sponge.

Arthur Look, it's solid metal.

He bangs it against the proscenium arch. The Musical Director makes a clanging sound but a beat late.

Let me show you that again.

He goes to bang it again but the clang happens before he's hit the arch.

(*To Musical Director.*) You're meant to do it at the same time. One more go.

He hits it and the clang happens at the same time.

(*Cod voice.*) As you can see, ladies and gentleman, it is solid steel.

The Chairman Get on with it.

Arthur I will now bend it with my bare hands.

He grits his teeth and uses all his might to bend the steel, accompanied by a sound effect from the band.

The Chairman Amazing.

Arthur throws the bent steel to one side. The Musical Director makes a clang noise a clear beat after it hits the floor.

Now watch as Sturdy Sid lifts the heaviest weight we could find.

There's an old-fashioned weighted bar with two black round weights on each end. Arthur psychs himself up. He bends down and grabs the bar. He grits his teeth and strains as he tries to lift it. He strains and strains but it's not budging.

Arthur (*aside, through gritted teeth*) I thought it was gonna be rubber like the steel bar.

The Chairman (*aside*) Oh no, we got the real thing.

Arthur I can't lift it.

The Chairman Get off then.

Arthur Sorry, folks.

A dejected Arthur sidles off.

The Chairman Oh, it's gonna be a long night. Don't you be feeling sorry for him, rest assured he'll be back.

Jack quickly rushes on and picks the weights up with one hand and carries them off on his shoulder.

SCENE ELEVEN

We go backstage. The other side of a large flat. Dora and Ellen are milling about. We can hear what's happening onstage.

The Chairman (*off*) Now it's time for the free and easies, your talent show. Where anyone can have a go at entertaining us.

Jack passes through with a long stripey hook and goes to the side of the stage.

Jack Stripey-hook time.

Ellen I love this.

Arthur joins them.

Arthur Maybe I'll get some ideas for a new act.

Dora You'll find something, I know you will.

Arthur, Ellen and Dora listen and watch the shadow play through the flat.

The Chairman (*off*) Who's up first? Come on then, Miss, Mrs, Mr, no it is a Miss . . . I'm not sure what she's going to do, ladies and gentlemen. Maybe juggle.

We see the silhouette of a woman, who starts juggling but drops the balls immediately. The band plays some accompanying music.

(*Off.*) Oh you've dropped them.

She picks them up and has another go. She drops them.

(*Off.*) And again . . . I can guess what's coming.

Audience Off, off, off.

We see the silhouette of the cane coming out. She picks up more balls and then drops them – the crowd cheering and clapping as it gets closer.

The Chairman (*off*) They don't seem to like you, love. It would help if you could actually keep the balls in the air . . .

The crowd cheers and boos more. The hook loops round her neck and swiftly pulls her off the stage.

Ellen She was terrible.

Dora I know – isn't it great?

More acts come and go, hooked off as the scene in the foreground continues. The next is a man with a large snake – we see his silhouette.

He's got a snake!

The Chairman (*off*) He looks scary.

Man with Snake (*off*) He's not really.

The Chairman (*off*) I was talking to the snake.

The act continues in the background. The Man with Snake wraps the snake around himself, as Arthur talks to Ellen and Dora.

Arthur I've got a new idea for this.

Ellen Here we go.

Arthur Instead of the stripey hook pulling them off when they're rubbish, we'd have four judges who watch the acts and if they don't like one they press down on this big wooden button, with a cross on it.

He takes out a big wooden button with a cross on it and presses it. He makes a raspberry noise. A flag with a cross comes down from up in the flies. It looks like one of the crosses from Britain's Got Talent.

Thanks, Alec. And then another and another.

Three more flags appear.

And if you get four you're off. What do you think?

Dora Naah.

Ellen It'll never catch on.

Arthur It's a terrible idea.

The Man with Snake is booed and hooked off on the stage.

Another act comes on – a group of awful acrobats trying to make a human pyramid.

Arthur and Dora busily move props about and leave.

Mr Charles appears out of nowhere – almost magically from behind some props or out of a sofa – next to Ellen.

Mr Charles I've been watching you.

Ellen Where the hell did you spring from?

Mr Charles Trapdoors everywhere. I can tell you're a classically trained actor.

Ellen Can you?

Mr Charles Of course.

Ellen By my deportment?

Mr Charles Is that what they call it?

Ellen Was it my vibrato?

Mr Charles I haven't seen that yet. I love the classical repertoire. Proper plays. *Troilus and Cressida, Medea* . . . *Charley's Aunt.*

Ellen You're a man after my own heart. My Freddie loved the classics. He was always encouraging me to try and lift the bar here. And I'm going to get my chance at last tonight, you'll see, but he won't . . .

Mr Charles He couldn't make it?

Ellen (*blunt*) He's dead, dear. I miss him so much, and the way I'm going it looks like I'll be joining him very soon. As this . . .

Mr Charles Is probably your last performance, yeah.

SCENE TWELVE

We go back on stage. The Chairman is ready for the next act.

The Chairman (*shouting off*) Maybe less eager with the hook next time? If you push on his hip bone it should go back in the socket. (*Back to audience.*) That's enough awful acts for now. Oh no. We've got one more for you. Only joking. Sort of. Dame Ellen Bloggs of Allerton has been begging me to do something classy, whether this is it I don't know. Here you are. Ear plugs available here.

Jack appears with his tray, this time with ear plugs and a sign saying EAR PLUGS 6d.
Dame Ellen comes on in full 'Ride of the Valkyries' mode – Viking helmet, spear and shield. She spots Jack and spears him in the bottom.

Jack Ow!

He dashes off. She sings.

I WANT TO SING IN OPERA

Ellen
I'm getting so tired of these comedy songs
I want to sing something divine
I'm sure and I'm certain to shine
As a star in the opera line
I simply love Wagner, Mozart ans Puccini
Their music is really tip-top
So I mean to change my name – Bloggs to Bloggini
And see if I can't get a 'shop'.

Mr Charles watches from the side of the stage. He loves it – crying with emotion.

Mr Charles Stupendous!

Ellen

> I want to sing in opera
> I've got that kind of voice
> I'd always sing in opera
> If I could have my choice
> Signor Caruso
> Told me I ought to do so
> That's why I want to sing in op'ra
> Sing in op-pop-pop-popera hurrah.
>
> I want to play Carmen, I just love the part
> The music's so awfully sweet
> And all prima donnas I beat
> If in *Faust* I played fair Marguerite
> I'd warble and trill like a human canary
> In recitative or duet
> But managers seem to be just a bit wary
> My chances hasn't happened as yet.

Chorus.

> I want to sing in opera
> I've got that kind of voice
> I'd always sing in opera
> If I could have my choice
> Signor Caruso
> Told me I ought to do so
> That's why I want to sing in op'ra
> Sing in op-pop-pop-popera hurrah.

Mr Charles Bravo, brava! A triumph my dear.

She's very emotional as she goes off. The Chairman reappears.

The Chairman Speechless.

We've got another new act for you now. Well he's not new, you've seen him before. Told you he'd be back. Your local man of many or no talents depending on your point of view. All the way from Egypt, via Ormskirk, I give

57

you, please take him, the Great Magico. That the best
you could come up with?

Egyptian music plays.
    *Arthur comes out wearing an Egyptian death mask
    with a large white hood and cloak. He moves about
    the stage with lots of dramatic flourishes.*
    He lifts the mask up.

Arthur Only me, folks. Nothing to worry about.

He puts the mask back over his face.
    *He takes out a small wooden pyramid. He opens the
    front, we see inside and that it's empty. He does a big
    flourish and throws some glitter over it. He reaches
    inside the pyramid and pulls out a handful of white
    feathers. He lifts up the mask and looks inside the
    pyramid.*

(*To offstage.*) I think it's dead. I'm not gonna try the
rabbit . . .

*He puts the mask back down and chucks the pyramid
    to one side. He brings on a large Proteus cabinet on
    wheels that is shaped liked a mummy's tomb. He
    shows it off with lots of drama – turning it round so
    we can see behind it.*
    *He tries to speak but it is all muffled through the
    mask.*
    The Chairman reappears.

The Chairman We can't hear you through that stupid
mask.

*Arthur shrugs his shoulders. He opens the front of the
    cabinet and we see that it's empty inside. Arthur and
    the Chairman put their hands through the sides of the
    cabinet – it's made out of strips of material – up and
    down to show that there's nothing inside. Arthur
    closes the door on the front, does more dramatic*

flourishes as the music climaxes. He opens the door and there's nothing inside.

The Chairman What a surprise.

Arthur looks inside and round the back confused. He shrugs again. He points to the Chairman and the audience.

Right, we need a volunteer from the audience. Anyone stupid enough to take part in a magic trick by someone who doesn't know what they're doing? And I'm not even gonna mention what happened in rehearsal. They think she might get her sight back in a couple of weeks . . .

Jack is in the audience, dressed in a Little Bo-Peep costume with golden ringlets. He reluctantly puts his hand up.

The Chairman Yes, young lady. You'll do.

Jack makes his way up to the stage.

Jack I don't know why I have to be dressed up as a girl.

The Chairman None of this makes any sense, so don't start picking it apart.

Jack And why a Little Bo-Peep costume?

The Chairman It's all they had, they spent all the budget on this box, now shut up.

Jack Dora better hadn't see me like this.

The Chairman shoves Jack inside the box.

The Chairman Who's the magician, me or him?

Arthur goes offstage. At this point to be replaced by a double in exactly the same costume while Arthur scarpers to the back of the theatre. Arthur Two comes back on with two large swords.

Bloomin' heck. You sure about this?

Arthur Two shakes his head.

Oh well, you do seem to have their attention for once.

*Arthur Two spears the side of the box with a sword.
A high-pitched scream from Jack.*

Jack Aaah!

The Chairman You okay in there?

Jack No.

The Chairman I'll get the first-aid box. (*To Arthur Two.*)
Hurry up and get on with it.

Arthur Two pierces the other side.

Jack Ow!

*Arthur Two pulls both swords out dramatically and
then with a big drum roll opens the front of the
cabinet to reveal that Jack has disappeared.*

The Chairman How did you do that?

*Arthur Two shrugs his shoulders.
He closes the cabinet again. He performs a little
sand dance to the music, then opens the cabinet to
reveal Ellen inside having a cup of tea, confused how
she got there.*

Ellen What the . . . ? I was having a cup of tea in the
green room.

She strolls off.

The Chairman Are you doing actual magic?

*Arthur Two shrugs his shoulders again. He closes the
cabinet – does another little sand dance, the Chairman
joining in this time. Arthur Two opens the cabinet
again, and Jack is there dressed as a mummy in
bandages.*

The Chairman He's doing magic!

Jack I don't care. At least I'm out of that dress.

Jack leaves as Arthur – dressed in his regular clothes – comes through the stalls with a Sayers pasty in his hand. He's confused and curious as to how there's another him on stage.

The Chairman I'm well impressed.

Arthur Two dances around very pleased with himself as Arthur joins the Chairman on stage. He turns to Arthur.

It's amazing, this is, Arthur.

He does a double-take.

Arthur? Then who's he?

Arthur I haven't the faintest idea. I just found myself in Ye Olde Sayers on Williamson Square. Got a meat and potato pasty out of it though.

The Chairman Who are you, eh, mate?

The Chairman takes the head off Arthur Two and it's Mr Charles underneath.

Mr Charles It's me!

The Chairman *and* **Arthur** You!

Mr Charles Wasn't that wonderful? I think I've found my calling. Signed autographs at stage door after the show.

He disappears.

The Chairman It wasn't even you. You can't do magic, you're still crap then?

Arthur That's a bit harsh. (*To the audience.*) Isn't it, ladies and gentlemen?

The Chairman Get off and take your cupboard with you.

*Arthur sadly wheels his cabinet off. The audience
hopefully feel sorry for him.*

(*To audience.*) Oh give over.

*Instrumental glimpse of 'I Was a Good Little Girl Till
I Met You' as we cross to the Number One Dressing
Room.*

SCENE THIRTEEN

*Ida is in her dressing room rifling through a large trunk
of her belongings.*
    She looks at a photo, holds it to her chest and cries.
    She takes out a large sombrero and cries some more.
    *She takes out a very girthy chorizo. She holds it in her
hand.*

Ida Alfonsssssooooo.

Dora comes in, Ida tries to cover.

Dora Ah, look at all your gorgeous things all the way
from . . . (*She reads a label on the trunk.*) Lloret de Mar.
That's so glamorous. Your life is so . . .

Ida Darling, it's not glamorous. It's hard work and
misery most of the time.

Dora But I thought you said . . .

Ida That's all part of the act, my dear. It's not just what
goes on out there on stage, it's all one bloody big
performance. Living out of a suitcase, a different
enchanting town every night. Bolton, Sutton Coldfield,
Aberystwyth . . . Why do you think I'm back?

Dora Because you're on a world tour? And you love it
here and miss the home crowd?

Ida My toreador dumped me. I was too old for him. Too past it. What was I thinking? It was just a pathetic holiday romance. And I'm skint. (*A glimpse of Scouse.*) I'm on the bones of me arse. (*Theatrical voice again.*) I've got nothing to my name apart from this trunk full of castanets and sand. I try to hold my head high but . . .

Jack appears.

Jack We're ready for you now, Miss Valentine.

She gets up and heads out.

Ida I really don't know what I'd do if I didn't have this . . .

SCENE FOURTEEN

The Chairman is back on stage.

The Chairman How we doing? Holding on? This one's gagging for a drink here. Nearly at the interval, you'll be pleased to hear.

Look at these ones in the expensive seats. From The Wirral, they've got interval drinks lined up and everything. They think it makes them look posh but it's just because they're hardened drinkers and they can't wait for their liquor. I've got your number, lady.

Here she is again. All the way from . . . (*Twitch of head.*) Spain. The venerable, veritable, veiny (ugh), vertical, sometimes vicious, sometimes vindictive, even violent, always vibrant, victorious, vigorous, visionary, vivid, vocal, vol-au-vent, voracious, vivid Miss Ida Valentine.

Ida Valentine comes out. A brief moment of warmth between them.

Ida Thank you, duckie.

The Chairman My pleasure, my sweet.

Ida I'm back. I didn't go far.

She sings.

A LITTLE OF WHAT YOU FANCY DOES YOU GOOD

Ida

I never was a one to go and stint myself
If I like a thing, I like it, that's enough
But there's lots of people say that if you like a thing
    a lot
It'll grow on you and all that sort of stuff
Now I like my drop of stout as well as anyone
But a drop of stout's supposed to make you fat
And there's many a la-di-da-di madam doesn't dare
    to touch it
Cos she mustn't spoil her figure, silly cat.

Chorus.

I always hold with having it if you fancy it
If you fancy it, that's understood
And suppose it makes you fat?
I don't worry over that
A little of what you fancy does you good.

*The Chairman spots Mr Charles at the side of the
stage.*

The Chairman Eh, I wanna talk to you.

He dashes after him.

Ida

Now, once a year I like a little holiday
And we've always had one, my old man and me
But the last time that we had one he brings up a
    new idea
As we watched the ladies bathing in the sea

64

He said what a man requires is a change of everything
So he ought to take his holidays alone
Right away from everyday affairs, so I said, very likely,
Well, if you prefer a fortnight on your own.

Chorus.
I always hold with having it if you fancy it
If you fancy it, that's understood
But if that's your bloomin' game
I intend to do the same
A little of what you fancy does you good.

We go backstage with the Chairman. He finds Mr Charles.
    Ida keeps singing onstage in the background.

The Chairman Who are you? What is your story?

Mr Charles Would you like to know?

Ellen and Arthur join too.

The Chairman Yeah, it's getting a bit strung out now and half-time's any minute.

Dora and Jack join.

Mr Charles Well, you know there's a new owner? That's me.

Arthur Really?

Ellen If only we'd put two and two together.

Mr Charles Even I could see it coming on page ten and I'm pissed the whole time.

The Chairman What are you going to do?

Mr Charles I'm just going to give it a lick of paint and put in some more women's loos.

Ellen (*to audience*) There's never enough, is there, girls?

The Chairman You're not much of a baddie then, are you?

Mr Charles Only kidding. I've got dastardly, evil, fiendish plans.

Ellen That's a shame, I thought we were getting on like a house on fire.

Mr Charles I've got a plan so unscrupulous it will make your teeth hurt and your toes curl.

The Chairman Terrifying.

Jack Horrific.

Arthur I'm gonna have nightmares.

Dora What's he talking about?

Arthur So what is it?

Mr Charles I'm going to close this place down.

Ellen No.

The Chairman You can't.

Mr Charles I can. I can do whatever I want. I'm a rich capitalist and you're just the lowly working class, get used to it. This is just the beginning. I imagine in the future us capitalists will be getting away with murder. Tax havens to hide all our filthy lucre and contracts of the zero hours – but I'm getting ahead of myself now.

Ellen When will you close us down?

Mr Charles Well, not yet. But very soon. After the interval. In Act Two. That's my plan.

The Chairman Despicable.

Arthur Nasty.

Jack Spiteful.

Mr Charles I know.

Dora I still don't know what's going on.

Jack I'll explain in the interval.

Dora Ta.

The Chairman What would we all do without The Star?

Mr Charles Not my problem. You can carry on with that jolly song now, knowing that things will never be the same again . . . Oo ah ha ha. Exit stage left. Always stage left.

He disappears. We go back onstage. Ida still singing.

Ida

I had to catch this certain train the other day
And I very nearly lost it, I declare
But the guard said, 'Jump in, missus,' then he shoved
    me in first class
And I found a nice young couple sitting there
I could see that honeymoon was stamped all over 'em
I felt sorry for the lady and the chap
So I said to them, 'Excuse me, but if you want to have
    a cuddle
Have a cuddle cos I'm going to have a nap.'

Chorus.

And I'm always always having it if you fancy it
Get on with it, don't waste my time
And while you young couples spoon
I'll dream I'm on my honeymoon
Cos a little of what you fancy does you good.

See you in twenty minutes. Ta-ra for now.

Curtain.

End of Act One.

Act Two

SCENE ONE

The band starts to play the intro of the next number. The Chairman's face appears spotlit on stage. We only see his face as he's in costume for the next number.

The Chairman You all come back? Hurry back from the urination facilities. Finish your ice creams. You all had a drink? I can see you have, madam. What was it this time? Sambuca? Tequila, rum and port? And a slice of lemon. Classy.

Ready for the next number?

Now a couple of our dancers are off, they've got a touch of TB. And gout. And croup, scurvy, rickets and diphtheria. So we've got certain persons standing in. You lucky people.

We're going to take you on a nautical adventure. Get your sea legs, we're off down the docks . . . Not that part of the docks. I know what you're thinking, love. This is a nice innocent show.

We're putting on a big show for you even though we think we're gonna close, but maybe we can defeat what's-is-face and stay open. Thought I'd throw in a bit of plot for you, keep it ticking along.

There's a nautical/seaside backdrop. Ellen starts to sing the first verse on her own.

Ellen (*during intro*) This will probably be my last performance.

SHIP AHOY

When the man-o'-war or merchant ship comes sailing
   into port

The jolly tar with joy, will sing out 'land ahoy'
With his pockets full of money and a parrot in a cage
He smiles at all the pretty girls upon the landing stage.

The rest of the cast appear dressed as sailors – Dora, Jack, then the Chairman and Arthur. They're in ill-fitting costumes and they can't do the choreography.

Chorus.
All the nice girls love a sailor
All the nice girls love a tar
For there's something about a sailor
Well, you know what sailors are
Bright and breezy, free and easy
He's the ladies' pride and joy
Falls in love with Kate and Jane
Then he's off to sea again
Ship ahoy, ship ahoy.

Ida slowly appears in a rowing boat pulled by Jack. Though he's struggling.

Ida I'm not that fat. Come on, get me on or I'll miss the whole bloody song.

The Chairman and Arthur appear and push her on from behind. She nearly falls out.

Careful! I don't wanna capsize.

ROW, ROW, ROW

Ida
Young Johnny Jones he had a cute little boat
And all the girlies he would take for a float
He had girlies on the shore
Sweet little peaches by the score
But Master Johnny was a wise 'un, you know
His steady girl was Flo
And every Sunday afternoon
She'd jump in his boat and they would spoon.

Chorus.

And then he'd row, row, row
Way up the river he would row, row, row
A hug he'd give her, then he'd kiss her now and then
She would tell him when
He'd fool around, and fool around
And then they'd kiss again
And then he'd row, row, row
A little further he would row. Oh! Oh! Oh! Oh!
Then he'd drop both his oars, take a few more encores
Then around by the reeds, he'd do more daring deeds
And then he'd row, row, row.

SHE SELLS SEA SHELLS

Ellen sings two choruses of 'She Sells Sea Shells'.

Ellen Come on, everyone, your turn. You all got your teeth in?

The words appear on a song sheet and she gets everyone to sing along to the chorus.

The cast have now all transformed into bathing beauties in old-fashioned full-coverage swimming costumes, bathing caps and beach balls. They form a line from front to back of the stage – Ida at the front.

OH I DO LIKE TO BE BESIDE THE SEASIDE

Ida

Everyone delights to spend their summer's holiday
Down beside the side of the silvery sea
I'm no exception to the rule
In fact, if I'd my way
I'd reside by the side of the silvery sea
But when you're just the common or garden Smith
    or Jones or Brown
At business up in town

You've got to settle down
You save up all the money you can till summer comes
    around
Then away you go
To a spot you know
Where the cockleshells are found.

*Ida steps out and each person is revealed behind her.
Ellen, then Dora, Jack and then Arthur looking
ridiculous, but then the Chairman looking even worse.*

The Chairman Why did I agree to this?

*They sing the song and perform a dance routine with
beach balls. The Chairman and Arthur all over the
place.*

Company (*chorus*)
Oh I do like to be beside the seaside
I do like to be beside the sea
I do like to stroll upon the prom, prom, prom
Where the brass bands play
Tiddly-om-pom-pom.

*The Chairman gets carried away and pulls his back
out. He limps off.*

So just let me be beside the seaside
I'll be beside myself with glee
And there's lots of girls besides
I should like to be beside
Beside the seaside, beside the sea.

SCENE TWO

*We go backstage as they leave the stage, and we hear the
Chairman introducing another act. Everyone else is
milling about, Jack running around as usual trying to
keep the show together.*

The Chairman (*off*) Still coming tonight, Zaeo, the human catapult. She'll be fired from the stage into the dress circle or somewhere thereabouts. She costs us a fortune in chandeliers.

Jack walks through with a huge catapult.

(*Off.*) Then we've got Tallulah and the trumpet-playing ferrets.

Jack Ferret on the loose!

Dora and Arthur scream. Jack picks up the Chairman's hammer and chases after a ferret across the floor. It then whizzes up and round the edge of the proscenium.

Get it!

The Chairman (*off*) We've got a treat in store for you now. One of our old favourites. Yes, her name's Elizabeth and she's a right cow, if I do say so myself. No, don't boo, ladies. She is actually a cow. Bring her on and let's guess the weight of the cow!

We hear a loud moo and see the silhouette of a large cow and her owner.
Ida nearly stands in a cowpat backstage.

Ida Eeh, what fresh hell is that?

Jack Watch out, everyone. She's left a trail. Don't stand in it.

He clears away a cowpat.

I could be working back on the farm again.

Dora laughs.
Ida and Ellen pass each other – all smiles.

Ellen (*aside*) Hussy.

Ida (*aside*) Moose.

72

Ida leaves. The Chairman comes backstage.

The Chairman I'll leave them to ponder on the beef for a bit. Has anyone seen our new owner?

Dora No sign of him.

Arthur The rotter.

The Chairman He could come and close us down tonight if he feels like it.

Ellen He'll have me to deal with if he tries. He'll not be shutting up shop here while I'm still alive, which might not be too long. This could be my last evening . . .

The Chairman If we see him let's all be friendly and try and encourage him to keep us open.

Ellen You can count on me.

Mr Charles comes backstage with his umbrella up – he's just come from outside and the rain.

Mr Charles It's raining Siamese and Chihuahuas out there.

Ellen sees this and starts freaking out.

Ellen Put. That. Umbrella. Down! Don't you know it's bad luck backstage . . .

Mr Charles Oh, I am sorry. I was just shielding my black cat from the rain.

He takes out a black cat.

Ellen Oh no.

Dora Ellen is very superstitious, you can't have anything that brings bad luck here.

Mr Charles And my pet magpie. (*To audience.*) I know this doesn't make much sense, but bear with.

He takes out a magpie.

Ellen Oh dear God.

Mr Charles I've actually got thirteen of them. At home.

Ellen Aargh!

The Chairman Whatever you do don't mention the Scottish play . . .

Mr Charles Did I ever tell you about the time I played Mac—

She punches him in the face and knocks him out.

The Chairman You're really being so nice and friendly to him, getting him onside.

Mr Charles slowly comes to.

Mr Charles But I only said that I played . . .

Ellen Say it once more and you're dead meat.

Ellen strolls off.

Mr Charles What just happened?

Dora and Jack look after Mr Charles and escort him off.
Ida passes through.

Ida Duckie?

The Chairman (*busy*) You're not on again just yet . . .

Ida Darling, now, Beverley . . .

The Chairman You know not to use my real name! Nobody knows, call me the Chairman.

Ida Your secret's safe with me.

The Chairman I don't know what my parents were thinking, three sons called Beverley, Lindsay and Hilary. The worst was our sister Ronald.

Ida I just wanted to have a little chit-chat . . .

He's distracted as usual.

The Chairman Now?

Ida I know you're busy . . .

The cow on stage moos.

With cows and magic and . . . I just wanted to say, I'm feeling so happy . . .

The Chairman This is you being happy?

Ida Yes. (*She puts on a big smile.*) See.

The Chairman Right.

Ida That's it, really. I'll let you get on.

The Chairman What's going on? Is this some sort of game? A trick?

Ida Me? Tricks! Games? Ha!

The Chairman The crowds *are* loving your return.

Ida I *love* this place. And it makes me think of me and you. This is where it all started. Us and The Star.

The Chairman A long time ago.

Ida But it feels like yesterday. I've been having the strangest thoughts. Maybe we were a good couple . . .

The Chairman Very strange.

Ida Lunacy.

The Chairman Madness.

Ida Insanity.

A loud long moo on stage.

The Chairman Oh, me cow.

He rushes off. Ida is left alone on stage.
She sings.

I WAS A GOOD LITTLE GIRL TILL I MET YOU

Ida

When I was young and innocent you stole into my
   heart
You taught me things I now repent whenever we're
   apart
You taught me that the world was wide, a bit too wide
   for me
And now I am not satisfied with just a cup of tea.

Chorus.

I was a good little girl till I met you
You sent my head in a whirl
My poor heart too
Oh how you told me the tale
You always do
I was a good little girl
Till I met you.

I never stayed out late at night, well, never after ten
To men I was indifferent quite until you came and then
You took me walking in the park, you talked like
   Romeo
And when you kissed me in the dark, poor me, I did
   not know.

Chorus.

I was a good little girl till I met you
You sent my head in a whirl
My poor heart too
Oh how you told me the tale
You always do
I was a good little girl
Till I met you.

76

Am I in love with him again? No. Maybe. Who'd have thought? Should I give him another chance?

She thinks.

SCENE THREE

The Chairman is back on stage.

The Chairman You know that saying 'God loves a trier'? I'd like to introduce a new phrase: 'God loves someone who knows when to call it quits.' You couldn't apply that to our next act, oh yes, he's still alive, he'll never die, he'll outlive the cockroaches. He's got a wallpapering act. He's going to put up some wallpaper. No doubt even less entertaining than watching paint dry. Arthur Crown.

Arthur appears in overalls and start wallpapering. There's a wallpapering table, brushes, buckets and a wall to paper.

Arthur You're gonna love this. First you lay your wallpaper out on a table. Then you get your wallpaper paste . . .

Audience Make us laugh.

Arthur Has anyone seen my coal scuttle?

Audience That's still not funny.

Arthur Maybe I could sing to you while I do this.

Audience Or just go home.

Arthur Maestro, please.

The band fails to strike up.

Please!

The band strike up. Arthur sings and the number develops into a slapstick wallpaper act.

77

Arthur

Our parlour wanted papering, Pa said it was waste
To call a paperhanger in and so we made some paste
He bought some rolls of paper a ladder and a brush
And with me mother's nightgown on at it he made
a rush.

Chorus.

When Father papered the parlour, you couldn't see Pa
for paste
Dabbing it here, dabbing it there, paste and paper
everywhere
Mother was stuck to the ceiling; the kids were stuck
to the floor
I never knew a blooming family so stuck up before.

*The Chairman joins in, with Arthur as the young
trainee who's useless at wallpapering, the Chairman as
the boss with bowler hat and cigar.*
    *Much confusion with planks, ladders, buckets of
wallpaper paste. Comedy double act – with Arthur
being inadvertently funny.*

The pattern was 'blue roses', its leaves red white and
brown
He'd stuck it wrong way up and now we all walk
upside down
And when he trimmed the edging off the paper with
the shears
The cat got underneath it and Dad cut off both its ears.

Chorus.

When Father papered the parlour, you couldn't see Pa
for paste
Dabbing it here, dabbing it there, paste and paper
everywhere
Mother was stuck to the ceiling; the kids were stuck
to the floor

I never knew a blooming family so stuck up before.

The Chairman We need a hand with this wallpapering.

Arthur Yes, another pair of hands.

The Chairman Who'd like to help? How about this young innocent lad?

Jack is in the audience.

Jack Why is it always me?

The Chairman Get up here.

Jack is wearing overalls.

Jack I've come prepared this time.

He starts to get tangled up in the wallpaper and covered in paste.

Arthur
    Soon Dad fell down the stairs and dropped his
        paperhanger's can
    On little Henrietta sitting there with her young man
    The paste stuck them together as we'd thought 'twould
        be for life
    We had to fetch the parson in to make them man and
        wife.

The words to the chorus appear on a large sheet of wallpaper/songsheet.

The Chairman All join in.

Chorus.
    When Father papered the parlour, you couldn't see Pa
        for paste
    Dabbing it here, dabbing it there, paste and paper
        everywhere
    Mother was stuck to the ceiling; the kids were stuck
        to the floor

I never knew a blooming family so stuck up before.

We're never going to move away from that house
   any more
For Father's gone and stuck the chairs and table to
   the floor
We can't find our piano though it's broad and rather
   tall
We think that its behind the paper Pa stuck on the wall.

Chorus.
   When Father papered the parlour, you couldn't see Pa
      for paste
   Dabbing it here, dabbing it there, paste and paper
      everywhere
   Mother was stuck to the ceiling; the kids were stuck
      to the floor
   I never knew a blooming family so stuck up before.

*A big climax with Jack and Arthur getting covered in
wallpaper paste and paper. The Chairman managing to
stay clean.*

The Chairman None on me. Perfect.

SCENE FOUR

*Backstage. Mr Charles is taking in his building. He has a
tape measure in hand and is making notes.*

Mr Charles (*singing*) 'I love my theatre. My lovely little
theatre. That's all mine, no one else's . . .'

   *Ellen finds him. He sees her and steps back, thinking
   she might get violent again.*

Ellen Don't worry, I won't go ballistic again. Unless you
do something unlucky like start whistling.

Mr Charles Like this?

He whistles.
A sandbag on a rope swings past from above and just misses his head.

What was that?

Ellen A sandbag from the flies.

Mr Charles Just from doing this?

He whistles again.
Another sandbag swings from the other direction and just misses his head.

Ellen Stop it! You'll have yourself killed. It's unlucky for a real reason because that's how we communicate to the stagehands in the flies, by whistling. Lots of stagehands used to be sailors and had worked on ships too. (*She turns to the audience.*) Educational and entertaining, this show.

Mr Charles I'm learning so much about theatre!

Ellen You must be really loaded to buy this place and all that champagne.

Mr Charles I am.

Ellen Can I ask how you made all your money?

Mr Charles I'm very proud. We capitalists are. I own Ye Olde Bargain Booze. I'm loaded from selling cheap liquor to poor people. Wonderful. That's why I drink so much. It's all just sitting there on the shelves. And I've got a serious drink problem.

Ellen I see.

Mr Charles I also own Ye Olde Sports of the Direct. Staff on contracts of the zero hours and running and jumping attire made in China and sold for three and six.

Ellen Right. Have you decided what you're going to do with this place?

Mr Charles Not yet. I've got a bit more of Act Two to drag it out in.

Ellen I thought so.

Mr Charles But there's so much space back here. (*He looks around.*) I'm seeing shelves, shelves, shelves, shelves, shelves, shelves, shelves. Shelves, shelves, shelves, shelves, shelves . . .

Ellen Lots of shelves?

Mr Charles Aha.

He takes out his tape measure and starts measuring things. He measures Ellen.

Ellen You're measuring me?

Mr Charles Yes. Just wondering how tall you are.

He writes it down on his pad.

That's a good length for a lady.

He scribbles something else down. Ellen looks over his shoulder at what he's written.

Ellen How dare you. You've just written down the word 'mutton'.

Mr Charles That's what I'm having for my supper.

Ellen Oh.

He wanders off, randomly measuring things with his tape measure.
The Chairman passes through.

I've done some snooping and I think he's going to turn this place into a big old shop with lots of . . . shelves.

The Chairman Oh no. What can we do?

Ellen I'm working on him, let's hope my health holds up.

Ida appears. She's looking for the Chairman.

Ida There you are. (*To Ellen.*) And you're still alive?

Ellen What's that buzzing noise? Has a wasp got in somewhere?

She heads off. Under her breath but wanting Ida to hear:

Slattern.

Ida (*aside*) Guttersnipe.

The Chairman Will you two pack it in?

Ida Anyhow, more important things. I think we should give it another try. You and me. Us.

The Chairman You are joking.

Ida You know why I really came back, don't you?

The Chairman Because you're skint?

Ida Well, there is that.

The Chairman And that toreador chucked you out.

Ida Details. I am sorry for running off with him, it was a huge mistake. Though I did love his chorizo.

She turns to the audience.

Hey, none of that. His family had a delicatessen. Filthy, the lot of you.

The Chairman Are you actually saying sorry?

Ida Sounds like it, doesn't it. It's quite strange and out of character. Even I'm surprised. Anyhow, I really came back because I love this place and my heart belongs here. And because of you. We both know we should reunite . . .

The Chairman I'm speechless . . .

Ida For once.

He tries to summon up the words. They won't come. He kisses her.

The Chairman You know that's why I invited you back. Let me take you out tonight. After the show, just the two of us. A pork pie, pickled egg and a pint like old times.

Ida So romantic.

The Chairman Meet you here backstage.

Ida I will see you here. On this exact spot.

She dashes off.

The Chairman Did that really happen?

SCENE FIVE

Back on stage. Arthur steps out with paper in his hands. The Chairman joins him.

The Chairman Here he is again. Some would say determined, I'd say desperate. What is it this time?

Arthur Paper-tearing.

The Chairman Thrilling.

Arthur A jaunty number to accompany me please, Maestro.

The band play a jolly number as Arthur merrily tears paper and swings his knees back and forth. Bits of paper fall on the floor.

Getting there.

The Chairman Talk amongst yourselves.

He continues to tear.

Arthur Not much longer.

The Chairman If they hadn't had enough of you already, they will have now. Come on.

Arthur Done!

He proudly holds up his finished torn paper – it's a mess.

Look! (*He looks at it – grasping at straws.*) It's a snowstorm . . .

The Chairman points to the exit. Arthur leaves.

The Chairman Jack, do you wanna come and sweep this mess up?

He picks a clump of paper that Arthur has dropped. He opens it out and it's an intricate band of people holding hands.

Aah. Maybe he's not totally useless.

Jack sweeps up the paper and we go backstage with him and segue into the next scene.

SCENE SIX

Backstage. Dora is there with her bag, getting ready to leave. The theatre is empty. It's dark apart from the large ghost light.

Jack Are we the last two here?

Dora Looks like it. I hate being backstage at night and it's all deserted. I get really spooked.

Jack You've got nothing to be scared of. Though there is a reason this is called the ghost light.

Dora Don't say it's because it's haunted.

Jack All theatres are. And this is the last light left on at all times. If it goes off, the ghosts will get us.

Dora Stop it.

The light flickers.

Oh no.

Jack It's okay, I'm here.

There are props and sound-effect tools about. There's a thunder sheet and a rain machine. Jack hits the thunder sheet with a large hammer – it makes a loud thunder noise. She jumps.

Dora Aargh! What's that?

Jack It's the thunder sheet.

Dora I nearly had a heart attack.

He turns the handle on the rain machine. She jumps again.

Oh my . . . I'm a nervous wreck. Stop it now.

A door bangs off in the distance. Dora jumps and rushes into Jack's arms.

What was that? I'm sorry, but I need someone to hold me when I get frightened.

Jack I'm not complaining.

Dora You've never seen a ghost, have you?

Jack Here? I'm not saying anything . . .

Dora Oh go on, I quite like being scared.

She continues to hold him.

Jack (*not holding back*) There's meant to be a few ghosts and spirits here. There's a man in a top hat and tails, a girl in a red dress and the worst, the headless woman. Ow.

She's gripping him tighter.

Dora Is that too much?

Jack It's fine. Just like in the Tower of London. Terrifying. There's your nails . . .

Dora I bet you there's even a song to go with it.

Jack You're not wrong there.

He sings.

WITH HER HEAD TUCKED UNDERNEATH HER ARM

Jack
In the Tower of London large as life,
The ghost of Anne Boleyn walks they declare.
For Anne Boleyn was once King Henry's wife,
Until he made the headsman bob her hair!
Ah, yes, he did her wrong, long years ago
And she comes up at night to tell him soooo!

You've got nothing to be scared of.

With her head tucked underneath her arm
She walks the Bloody Tower
With her head tucked underneath her arm
At the midnight hour.

Oh, you're shaking.

Dora I'm not surprised.

Jack
She comes to haunt King Henry,
She means to give him 'what for',
Gadzook! She's going to tell him off

87

For having split her gore,
And just in case the headsman
Wants to give her an encore,
She has her head tucked underneath her arm.

Dora starts to laugh and lighten up. She climbs into a rail of costumes hanging up, and into a large dress with a ruff. Jack puts his head under the arm like a headless person. She laughs about and joins in the chorus.

Jack *and* **Dora**

With her head tucked underneath her arm
She walks the Bloody Tower
With her head tucked underneath her arm
At the midnight hour.

Dora puts her head at the top of the ruff – Jack's head still under the arm – and walks forward. But then she steps away and the dress seems to have a headless life of its own.

Jack

Along the draughty corridors,
For miles and miles she goes.
She often catches cold, poor thing,
It's cold there when it blows.
And it's awfully awkward for the queen,
To have to blow her nose,
With her head tucked underneath her arm.

Jack *and* **Dora**

With her head tucked underneath her arm
She walks the Bloody Tower
With her head tucked underneath her arm
At the midnight hour!

The dress with a life of its own disappears back into the clothes rail. The song finishes.

Jack There's no ghosts. You've nothing to worry about. Only playing.

Dora I know, I know.

The lights flicker on the ghost light and wind blows through the building. Doors slam. There's an eerie noise like a moaning.

Jack What the . . .?

They see a huge shadowy figure coming towards them out of the darkness. They hold each other for safety. It continues to make a moaning sound but then coughs and clears its throat. It's Ida, out of costume.

Ida Ooh, me throat. I should really cut down on the fags. What are you two lovebirds doing?

They jump apart like they've been caught.

Jack I'd better get on with my work.

He dashes off.

Ida Have you seen the Chairman? He's taking me out. We're getting back together.

Dora Oh, I'm made up for y'.

Ida It's all clear. He's the love of my life. I know we'll spend the rest of our lives together.

The Chairman appears across the other side of the stage talking to someone, his back to her.

There he is now.

Dora Have a great night, Miss Valentine.

She dashes off.

Ida (*whispering across, sing-song*) Duckie. Sweetheart.

He can't hear her. We now see who he's talking to –
a woman in a fancy dress and large hat. We can just
see the back of her.

The Chairman The hat's perfect.

Ida Who's he talking to?

The Chairman You look beautiful. The most beautiful
woman in Liverpool.

The woman giggles coquettishly.

Ida (*scouse*) The scoundrel. I'll show him . . .

She moves to walk forward to have it out but turns
instead.

Forget it.

She storms out of the theatre.

The Chairman So beautiful.

The woman laughs delicately again, then coughs and
lets out a big manly laugh. She turns and we see it's
Arthur dressed as a woman. A very pretty dress and
hat but awful make-up with big thick glasses on. The
Chairman starts laughing too.

Beautiful? You look awful!

Arthur But the audience will love it. I love it, especially
this Chinese silk. Feels lovely.

The Chairman We'll see. You are actually making me
laugh for once.

Arthur Maybe I've found my new act. What shall we call
her? Dolores?

The Chairman Oh, it's time for me to meet Ida. I said I'd
see her here now.

Arthur I hope she doesn't stand you up.

He clacks off in his heels.

These heels are killing me.

The Chairman She wouldn't do that. Would she? Where is she?

He waits. And waits. And waits.
  The lights fade.

SCENE SEVEN

The next day. Bright sunlight streams from the open back door, off.
  Mr Charles sits in the empty backstage with a small toy theatre. He plays with different doll actors – opening and closing the little red curtains. He's in a world of his own and acting out Hamlet with a figure, it seems. Ellen appears behind him.

Mr Charles To be or not to be, that is the question. Whether it is nobler to drink on an empty stomach or have a ham sandwich first . . .

Ellen Aah, look at that. You've got a toy theatre?

Mr Charles I had one when I was a child. Played with it all day long. Putting on my own little shows and productions.

Ellen Entertaining all your friends?

Mr Charles I didn't have any friends. It was just me . . . and the voices in my head.

Ellen Right. So you *do* love theatre?

Mr Charles I'd put on shows, plays, ballets and operas. I was so happy.

Ellen (*aside*) I think we're going to be all right after all . . .

Mr Charles Then one day I'd had enough and smashed it to smithereens.

Ellen Oh dear. It wasn't this one then?

Mr Charles No, this is for illustrative purposes only. But I don't need it either because now I've got a real one to play with. It's all mine. All mine . . .

He strolls off.

Ellen (*shouting after him*) Maybe you could keep it as a theatre? (*She thinks.*) Or he could smash this to smithereens. Is he going to knock it down? The mystery continues. Or drags, depending on your point of view and if you wanna get down the pub.

SCENE EIGHT

Dora in the dressing room. Ida comes in to get ready. She's in a foul mood – banging and crashing things about.

Ida 'The most beautiful woman in Liverpool'.

Dora Got the white dress ready for the waiting at the church number?

Ida He's gonna be waiting at the friggin' church. What a snake.

Dora Is there something wrong, Miss?

Ida If he thinks I'm going on there dressed as a bloody virginal bride he can take a running jump. Rat.

Dora (*aside*) Even I can see there's something wrong and I haven't a clue most of the time.

Ida I'm not singing that. I'm not going on. Toad.

Jack Your two-minute call, Miss Valentine.

Ida I'm fuming. Steaming. Hysterical!

Dora Are you going on?

She shrugs her shoulders.

Ida Wait until I see him. (*She sings.*) 'Two lovely black eyes . . .'

Jack Is she going on?

Ida I know. Too right I am. (*She rifles through a drawer and find some song sheets.*) I know.

SCENE NINE

The Chairman on stage.

The Chairman We've got Brian's Boxing Baboons coming. And of course Jessica Queen of the slack wire, with her wire that is slack . . . Got another treat in store for you now. She *is* here, I hear . . . (*Quiet.*) Even though she stood me up last night. Less said about that the better . . . The beautiful, buxom, brilliant . . .

Jack appears and whispers to The Chairman.

We might have a slight change to the advertised programme, ladies and gentlemen.

A crash from backstage.

I haven't the foggiest . . .

A scream of anger from backstage.

Ida Aargh! What a pig!

The Chairman Welcome the explosive, dynamite, hazardous, Mount Vesuvius, tornado, tsunami, that is Ida Valentine.

The band start playing the intro to 'Waiting at the Church'.
Ida comes out.

Ida Change of plan. We're doing these.

She hands over the sheet music to the band.
She sings.

WHO WERE YOU WITH LAST NIGHT?

Ida sings 'Who Were You With Last Night?' – about a man who's been seen with a mysterious woman.

The Chairman I don't know what's going on.

Ida Here's another old favourite for a certain person . . .

HOLD YOUR HAND OUT, NAUGHTY BOY

Ida
Hold your hand out, naughty boy
Hold your hand out, naughty boy
Last night in the pale moonlight
I saw you, I saw you
With a nice girl in the park
You were strolling full of joy
And you told her you'd never kissed a girl before
Hold your hand out, naughty boy.

Thank you, ladies and gentlemen, for your time and love.

She dashes offstage.

SCENE TEN

Backstage.
The Chairman catches Ida.

The Chairman What the hell was that all about?

Ida Did you listen to the words?

The Chairman I did, yeah, and . . .

Ida (*in Scouse*) Then it's plain as that fat nose on your face.

The Chairman What happened to 'Let's give it another try'? And were were *you* last night?

Ida Don't talk to me. Warthog!

She storms off. Chaos grows around him.

Jack Jessica Queen of the slack wire's gone crazy. She won't go on. She says her wire's too taut, it's not slack enough.

Dora passes through.

Dora Bill's in the audience with that one. Can you chuck them out for me?

Jack I'll chuck him out and box his ears!

The Chairman I need your help here. Who else we got? What about the clog-dancing badgers?

Arthur comes on dressed a billiard table with large pockets on his shoulders and waist.

Arthur If Dolores doesn't work, how about this?

He tries to make himself into a table – it's tricky.

Ellen I'm feeling most peculiar. I think I may join my Freddie any minute.

Mr Charles I need to talk to you about rats. I hear you've got lots of rats.

Jack The badgers have escaped.

Mr Charles That will sort out the rats.

Arthur Johnny Pocket, the human billiard table.

Ellen I won't even get through my song.

Dora I don't wanna see them . . .

Arthur What do you think, eh? Maybe back to Dolores?

Ellen Smelling salts . . .

Something furry runs across.

Jack There's a badger with clogs on.

Dora screams.
  Chaos.

The Chairman Aaaahhhh!

The intro starts and everyone fades into the background. They become undertakers and mourners at his funeral.

AIN'T IT GRAND TO BE BLOOMIN' WELL DEAD?

The Chairman sings 'Ain't It Grand to Be Bloomin' Well Dead?' – a song about wishing he was dead and imagining his own funeral.

The Chairman Oh, I feel a bit better after that.

Ellen comes by, looking out of sorts.

Talking of the dead.

Ellen Ugh, I'm not feeling well at all.

The Chairman That's not like you. (*Playful.*) Could tonight be your last performance?

Ellen You know I actually think it . . .

She collapses. The Chairman is unsure at first.

The Chairman This is a new one.

She doesn't get up.

You're really ill. (*He rushes over to her.*) Ellen, Ellen . . .
Is there a doctor in the house?

Arthur / Doctor (*off*) Yes!

*Arthur comes on dressed as a comedy doctor with
white coat, stethoscope, round mirror on his forehead
and doctor's bag.*

The Chairman Not you! A real one.

*Jack rushes on to help. Scenery is flown in to try and
hide her. It's all chaotic and messy.*

SCENE ELEVEN

*The Number One Dressing Room. Dora is getting
costumes ready. Ida stares into the mirror deep in thought.*

Dora (*humming along to herself*) 'I'm Bert, perhaps
you've heard of me, Bert . . .' This is one of me favourites.

Ida I bet you know all the words, don't you?

Dora To what?

Ida That song you were just singing.

Dora Which song? Your last performance of the night
now.

Ida I can't go on. What have I come back for? Why did
I do it? It was terrible idea.

Dora But they're waiting for y'.

Ida I don't care. Someone else will have to go on.

Dora Who?

Ida I wonder. Someone near here. In this room.

Dora looks round.

Dora Who?

Ida I forget, I can't be even the slightest bit cryptic with you.

She drags her behind a screen and changes her into the 'Bert' costume – which is a man's suit and hat.

Dora Me?

Ida Why not?

Dora I'm not ready.

Ida You couldn't be readier.

Dora But . . .

Ida You've always wanted to perform, haven't you?

SCENE TWELVE

On stage. The intro to 'Burlington Bertie' plays. No one appears. It plays again.

The Chairman Don't ask me what's going on tonight . . .

Ida pushes Dora out onto the stage. She gulps.

BURLINGTON BERTIE FROM BOW

Dora I'm Bert . . .

She freezes. She looks out into the crowd. The band stops playing.

I can't do it.

Jack appears at the side of the stage.

Jack You can do it. You know you can.

Dora I thought I could but . . .

Jack You can. You've always wanted to do this. It's your big chance. The audience love you. And . . . I love you.

He's shocked he's said it and tries to take it back.

What I meant to say was . . .

She looks at him half shocked, but it's just what she needs.

Dora Shush. Ready, band?

She gets into position, standing like Bert. The band starts up and she smashes it – starting small but then growing into the song and performance.

I'm Bert, perhaps you have heard of me,
Bert, you've had word of me
Jogging along, hearty and strong
Living on plates of fresh air
I dress up in fashion and when I'm feeling depressed
I shave from my cuff, all the whiskers and fluff
Stick my hat on and toddle up West.

I'm Burlington Bertie, I rise at ten-thirty
And saunter along like a toff
I walk down The Strand with my gloves on my hand
Then I walk down again with them off
I'm all airs and graces, correct easy paces
So long without food I forgot where my face is
I'm Bert, Bert, I haven't a shirt
My people are well off, you know
Nearly everyone knows me from Smith to Lord
    Rosebery
I'm Burlington Bertie from Bow.

My pose, though ironical
Shows that my monocle
Holds up my face, keeps it in place
Stops it from slipping away
Cigars, I smoke thousands, I usually deal in The Strand
But you've got to take care, when you're getting them
    there
Or some idiot might step on your hand.

I'm Burlington Bertie, I rise at ten-thirty
Then Buckingham Palace I view
I stand in the yard while they're changing the guard
And the King shouts across 'Toodle-oo'
The Prince of Wales' brother, along with some other
Claps me on the back and says 'Come and see Mother'
I'm Bert, Bert, and royalty's hurt,
When they ask me to dine I say 'No
I've just had a banana with Lady Diana
I'm Burlington Bertie from Bow.'

*The crowd goes wild. Flowers thrown on stage by
Jack.*

SCENE THIRTEEN

The Chairman finds Mr Charles backstage.

The Chairman I can't take much more tonight. Right,
you. Before you skulk off again I wanna know what
you're up to. Are you going to close us down and turn
us into a Ye Olde Land of the Pound?

Mr Charles Oh no, I've got a much better plan. I'm
going to turn this place into a proper theatre that only
does five-hour productions of Shakespeare. Starting with
the unfunny comedies, through the Henrys and then
maybe *Titus Andronicus*, all in Latin.

The Chairman That's evil.

Mr Charles I know. My plan is to alienate all the working-class people who come here now and make theatre just for poshos like me. Because, you know, music hall is innately inferior to legitimate theatre and that the working man, or woman – apparently some women work now – can only appreciate or comprehend entertainment as undemanding as this . . .

The Chairman That's offensive.

Mr Charles I know. The best part is that I'm going to be in all the productions. My *Midsummer Night's Dream* is a delight, wait until you see my Bottom.

The Chairman I'm saying nothing.

Mr Charles Or my one-man version of *The Tempest*, where I get to play a ship and a storm at the same time.

He demonstrates.

The Chairman It sounds awful.

Mr Charles Let me elaborate.

The Chairman Your turn to sing?

Mr Charles I haven't had a song in Act Two yet. Lock the doors.

THE NIGHT I APPEARED AS MACBETH

Mr Charles
'Twas through a YMCA concert
I craved a desire for the stage
In Flanders one night I was asked to recite
Gadzooks I was quickly the rage
They said I was better than Irving
And gave me some biscuits and tea
I know it's not union wages

But that was the usual fee
Home I came – bought a dress
Appeared in your theatre and what a success.

Chorus.
I acted so tragic the house rose like magic
The audience yelled 'You're sublime'
They made me a present of Mornington Crescent
They threw it a brick at a time
Someone threw a fender which caught me a bender
I hoisted a white flag and tried to surrender
They jeered me, they queered me
And half of them stoned me to death
They threw nuts and sultanas, fried eggs and bananas
The night I appeared as Macbeth.

Is Dame Ellen about?

The Chairman No, you're safe. I think we're okay in a song and 'The Scottish Play' doesn't scan so well.

Mr Charles
The advertised time for the curtain
Was six forty-five on the sheet
The hall keeper he having mislaid the key
We played the first act in the street
Then somebody called for the author
'He's dead' said the flute player's wife
The news caused an awful commotion
And gave me the shock of my life
Shakespeare dead – poor old Bill
Why I never knew the poor fellow was ill.

Chorus.
I acted so tragic the house rose like magic
I gave them such wonderful thrills
My tender emotion caused such a commotion
The dress circle made out their wills
The gallery boys straining, dropped tears uncomplaining

The pit put umbrellas up, thought it was raining
Some floated – some boated
And five of the band met their death
And the poor programme women
Sold programmes while swimming
The night I appeared as Macbeth.

The Chairman Sounds to me like you're a terrible actor.

Mr Charles Hmm, I didn't come out of that ditty too well, did I?

The Chairman And it sounds like you've got a terrible plan.

Mr Charles I shall not be dissuaded from my mission. I think I might be sobering up, where's the drink?

He wanders off.

The Chairman What am I gonna do? Let me take one last long look at the place.

He sits down on a big wicker basket at the back of the stage and takes in the place for the last time. He watches all the comings and goings.
A miserable Jack wheels across a trolley full of props. Dora finds him. She's still in the Burlington Bertie man's suit.

Dora Jack, Jack. I need to speak to you.

Jack I'm not in the mood, Dora. I feel daft.

Dora Do y'? Ah. I've got great news. I've gotta tell y'. I'm going on a date.

Jack Oh brilliant. Just rub it in a bit more. Who is it this time? Some rough burly sailor with tattoos? A local footballer? And why are you telling me?

Dora I'm telling you because . . . (*She's forgotten.*) Why am I telling y'?

Jack Well, I don't know.

Dora Because it's you. Me and you are going on a date.

Jack Since when?

Dora Now. I know it's quite forward, a girl asking a boy out, but you know, times are changing . . . That's if you want to.

He is open-mouthed. Speechless.

Dora Maybe you don't.

Jack Of course I do. I'd love to.

Dora I've been looking for love all this time and it was right in front of me.

Jack (*about time*) Er, yeah!

They look into each other's eyes and share a gentle kiss. Ida appears.

Ida About bloody time too. Though how you can be all smoochy smoo when my heart is broken, shattered into a thousand pieces, has been stamped on and squashed into the ground . . .

The Chairman is watching. He steps forward to join Ida just as Arthur appears at the front of the stage in his female attire, wearing a wedding dress and veil. Ida spots 'her'.

Ida There she is! The bitch. And in a friggin' wedding dress!

The Chairman What is it now?

Ida The bird, the judy, you've been going behind my back with.

The Chairman You've lost it this time.

Ida I saw you together. I heard you saying she was the most beautiful woman in Liverpool. Did you not say that?

The Chairman I did.

He laughs.

Ida You're brazen. Callous. This isn't funny. I knew it was a huge mistake to come back here.

The Chairman (*shouts across*) Oh Dolores, I'd like to have a word with you.

Ida Dolores? I've heard it all now.

Arthur (*in high-pitched voice*) Of course, my sugar plum.

Ida (*in Scouse*) Don't bring her over 'ere cos I'll rag her.

Arthur comes over. She can't see his face yet. He turns and lifts the veil.

Arthur (*deep voice*) Hiya.

Ida is open-mouthed.

Ida It's even worse than I imagined.

Arthur It's me – Arthur.

He lifts his glasses up.

Ida You what? You and him, her, him are a couple?

The Chairman Don't be daft.

Arthur It's me new act. Dolores, 'nosy neighbour'. I'm trying a new catchphrase, 'You been messing with my guttering?'

The Chairman What did you think?

Ida Of course, I knew that's what you were up to. (*Trying to be playful*). Well, I hope you're not going to try and steal any of my numbers. I feel a bit foolish now.

The Chairman You know you're the only woman for me.

Ida And you're the only fella.

Ellen appears in her most beautiful dress, large hat and pearls. But she's very pale and looking weak.

Arthur Ellen, what's wrong? You look awful.

Ellen (*about Arthur*) Who's she?

She nearly falls. She steadies herself.

The Chairman You shouldn't be here. You should have stayed at home in bed.

Ellen I haven't been feeling right for a while. I want to perform one last time.

Dora But you can hardly stand.

Ellen Before I go the great music hall in the sky. Before I join my Freddie.

Ida You can't go out like this.

Ellen Watch me. (*To the Chairman.*) Introduce me.

SCENE FOURTEEN

The Chairman comes out on to the stage to introduce Ellen.

The Chairman It's the incomparable, impressive, inspiring, indestructible, immaculate, idiosyncratic, oh yeah, indomitable, I don't know what that means either, irreplaceable, Dame Ellen Bloggs of Allerton . . .

A weak Ellen steps out on the stage. She's full of emotion.
The Chairman watches from the side of the stage.

Ellen (*sincere*) This will probably be my last performance.

Ellen

> I'm a young girl and have just come over
> Over from the country where they do things big
> And amongst the boys I've got a lover
> And since I've got a lover, why I don't care a fig.

Ida, Dora and Jack watch from the side of the stage.

Chorus.

> The boy I love is up in the gallery
> The boy I love is looking down at me
> There he is, can't you see, waving of his handkerchief
> As happy as the robin that sits in the tree.

Mr Charles appears at the side of the stage.

Mr Charles Dame Ellen. No, it can't be over.

Ellen

> The boy that I love, they call him a cobbler
> But he's not a cobbler allow me to state
> For Johnny is a tradesman and he works in the boro'
> Where they sole and heel them whilst you wait.

She's becoming weaker. Her voice crackling.

Chorus.

> The boy I love is up in the gallery
> The boy I love is looking down at me
> There he is, can't you see, waving of his handkerchief
> As happy as the robin that sits in the tree.

Mr Charles I was wrong. The Star Music Hall must stay open. In honour of the star of The Star, Dame Ellen.

The Chairman Yes!

Ellen

> Now if I were a duchess and had a lot of money
> I'd give it to the boy that's going to marry me

But I haven't got a penny so we'll live on love and
 kisses
And be just as happy as the birds in the tree.

*The whole gang all join her on the last chorus and
hold her as she starts to fade. Ida takes her hand at one
point – a small moment of connection and apology.*
 *Ellen gets one last burst of energy from them
supporting her.*

Chorus.
The boy I love is up in the gallery
The boy I love is looking down at me
There he is, can't you see, waving of his handkerchief
As happy as the robin that sits in the tree.

Ellen slowly leaves the stage and the lights dim.

ENCORE

Ida That was a bit of a downer, wasn't it?

The Chairman Shall we have a jolly one to finish off?

The church set for 'Waiting at the Church' flies in.
 Music starts with the Wedding March.
 *Jack and Dora walk forward arm in arm like they're
walking down the aisle of a church – Dora with a posy
of flowers. They stop at the front of the stage/altar.*
 *The Chairman and Ida do the same – Ida with
flowers.*
 *Arthur/Dolores walks down as the bride – veil
down, large posy.*
 Mr Charles watches from the side.
 Arthur/Dolores lifts the veil.

Arthur
    I'm in a nice bit of trouble, I confess
    Somebody with me has had a game
    I should by now be a proud and happy bride
    But I've still got to keep my single name
    I was proposed to by Obadiah Binks, in a very
        gentlemanly way
    Lent him all my money so that he could buy a home
    And punctually at twelve o'clock today . . .

Mr Charles Is this where the phrase 'spare prick at a wedding' originated?

Chorus.
    There was I, waiting at the church
    Waiting at the church, waiting at the church
    When I found he'd left me in the lurch
    Lor', how it did upset me
    All at once he sent me round a note
    Here's the very note, and this is what he wrote
    'Can't get away to marry you today,
    My wife won't let me.'

Ellen comes back out dancing.

Ellen I'm not really dead. It's my comeback tour!

Chorus.
    There was I, waiting at the church
    Waiting at the church, waiting at the church
    When I found he'd left me in the lurch
    Lor', how it did upset me
    All at once he sent me round a note
    Here's the very note, and this is what he wrote
    'Can't get away to marry you today,
    My wife won't let me.'

Mr Charles I don't think we've met, my dear. What's your name?

Arthur (*with a twinkle*) Dolores. Pleased to meet you.

Chorus.
     There was I, waiting at the church
     Waiting at the church, waiting at the church
     When I found he'd left me in the lurch
     Lor', how it did upset me
     All at once he sent me round a note
     Here's the very note, and this is what he wrote
     'Can't get away to marry you today,
     My wife won't let me.'

The End.

Composers and Lyricists

Don't Dilly-Dally
Words and music by Charles Collins and Fred W. Leigh

Down at the Old Bull and Bush
Words and music by A.B. Sterling, R. Hunting, P. Krone,
H. Von Tilzer

The Spaniard that Blighted My Life
Words and music by Billy Merson

When I Take My Morning Promenade
Words by A.J. Mills, music by Bennett Scott

Oh What a Beauty!
Words and music by Edrich Siebert

Are We to Part Like This, Bill?
Words and music by Harry Castling and Charles Collins

Champagne Charlie
Original lyrics by George Leybourne, music by Alfred Lee. Revised
lyrics by Ernest Irving and Frank Eyton

The Rest of the Day's Your Own
Words and music by Worton David and J.P. Long

I Want to Sing in Opera
Words and music by Worton David and George Arthurs

A Little of What You Fancy Does You Good
Words and music by Fred W. Leigh and George Arthurs

Ship Ahoy
Words by A.J. Mills, music by Bennett Scott

Row, Row, Row
Words by William Jerome, music by Jimmie V. Monaco

She Sells Sea Shells

Words by Terry Sullivan, music by Harry Gifford

Oh I Do Like to Be Beside the Seaside
Words and music by John A. Glover–Kind

I Was a Good Little Girl Till I Met You
Words by Clifford Harris, music by James W. Tate

When Father Papered the Parlour
Words and music by R.P. Weston and Fred Barnes

With Her Head Tucked Underneath Her Arm
Words and music by R.P. Weston, Bert Lee and Harris Weston

Who Were You With Last Night?
Words and music by Fred Godfrey and Mark Sheridan

Hold Your Hand Out, Naughty Boy
Words and music by C.W. Murphy and Worton David

Ain't It Grand to Be Bloomin' Well Dead?
Words and music by Leslie Sarony

Burlington Bertie from Bow
Words and music by William Hargreaves

The Night I Appeared as Macbeth
Words and music by William Hargreaves

The Boy I Love Is Up in the Gallery
Words and music by George Ware

Waiting at the Church
Words by Fred W. Leigh, music by Henry E. Pether